THE
OFFICIAL CANDIDATE'S
BOOK OF

Political Insults

THE
OFFICIAL CANDIDATE'S
—— BOOK OF ——

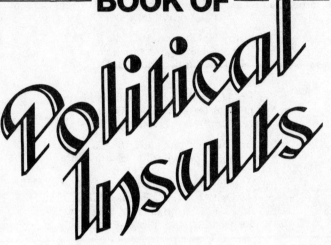

Political Insults

GRAHAM JONES

CENTURY

LONDON   MELBOURNE   AUCKLAND   JOHANNESBURG

Cartoons by Bill Belcher
Copyright © Graham Jones 1987

First published in 1987 by Century Hutchinson Ltd,
Brookmount House, 62–65 Chandos Place, Covent Garden,
London WC2N 4NW

Century Hutchinson Australia Pty Ltd,
PO Box 496, 16–22 Church Street,
Hawthorn, Victoria 3122
Australia

Century Hutchinson New Zealand Limited,
PO Box 40–086, Glenfield, Auckland 10,
New Zealand

Century Hutchinson South Africa (Pty) Ltd,
PO Box 337, Bergvlei 2012, South Africa

Set in 10/11pt Linotron Palatino
Photoset by Deltatype Ltd, Ellesmere Port, Cheshire
Printed and bound in Great Britain by
Richard Clay Ltd, Bungay, Suffolk

British Library Cataloguing in Publication Data

Jones, Graham, *1951–*
The official candidate's book of political
insults.
1.   Political satire
I.   Title
320'.0207   JA66

ISBN 0 7126 1482 6

Contents

Caustic Comment

'I am writing a book on political invective,' I whispered to the Prime Minister. 'I suppose you don't happen to collect political jokes yourself?' 'As a matter of fact I do,' she replied in a small, shrill voice. 'I've got a Cabinet full of them.'

Do not be deceived. Only my little political joke. This book is, in fact, in *praise* of politicians, which may make it something of a collector's item in itself, though the laudation is in a very specific direction. For nowhere can the art of cut-and-thrust, scorn, wit and repartee be better seen than among the men and women who daily shape our destiny. They are simply the masters of insult and invective. Not wholesale *abuse*, mind—though there is a lot of that about. This book is intended to be fun first.

That is, of course, how I flattered so many MPs, peers and trade union leaders to contribute to this book, right up to one party leader who contributed non-attributively. Let me declare an interest. I *like* politicians, and would even dare to count some among my friends. In 1985 this symbiotic relationship was allowed to flourish when I was sent by the *Daily Telegraph* to the House of Commons as a Lobby Correspondent.

During the period roughly bordered by the Brecon and Radnor by-election and Mr Colin Moynihan's extravagant MPs Thames bathe-in, I had privileged access to MPs and Cabinet Ministers, even meeting on occasions the Prime Minister herself. Naturally, I was to develop a taste for the finer points of politics, such as the sartorial elegance of Mr Gerald Kaufman and the breadth of the smile on the face of the PM's press supremo, Mr Bernard Ingham. It was a happy time, interrupted only by fourteen-hour periods of solid hard work most weekdays.

But there is something about being on the *inside* of the great decision-making process. One leading Cabinet 'wet' told me how he had disagreed with Lord Stockton's remarks about the Government 'selling off the family silver'. 'They've not just sold off the silver, they've sold off the hardwood furniture as well.' Another Minister told me how Leon Brittan's trouble was that his face always looked like he was wearing a stocking mask. I discovered that politicians really do hate each other, and in inverse proportion to the affinity of their views. At a lunch foursome, two unfortunate words were spoken to a leading SDP figure who suddenly began stabbing violently at a segment of lemon with a fork, as if having a rush of blood to the head during bayonet practice. The piece of lemon was then raised to the mouth and sucked avidly in something like the reverse of the kiss of life. The two offending words had been 'Roy Hattersley'.

I was delighted at the response when I asked a number of professional politicians whether they would contribute material for this book. Some invited me to the House to mull over the matter in convivial surroundings. With the irrepressible Mr Nicholas Fairbairn this involved generous Pimm's on the Commons Terrace and the chance to witness the Fordell Laird's considerable talent for impersonating his fellows.

One senior back-bencher kindly sent me a box of cigars to improve the mental process, while the ever-efficient Mrs Edwina Currie dispatched so much material it would best be described as a parcel. (I found it difficult to thank her, so determined is she to have the last word. My letter of gratitude brought an acknowledgement. I got the impression that if I acknowledged this, she would acknowledge my acknowledgement and set up a lifetime's correspondence.)

It is only fair to report that a number of MPs did not wish to make a contribution. Mr Tony Benn wrote that he candidly believed 'personal invective, though very funny, is calculated to discourage people from an interest in real politics'. This reminds me of taking tea with Mr Benn at Ystradgynlais during the Brecon and Radnor by-election campaign. I gently suggested to Mr Benn that Neil Kinnock might not have been very keen to have him there. This brought a long lecture to the effect that politics was about issues, not personalities. I listened with interest as Mr Benn spoke shortly afterwards. He had always believed that politics was about issues, not personalities, he began. But one man had made it inevitable that he mention his name. . . . The 'non-personalities' purist then launched into an extended denunciation of Dr David Owen.

Another rejection came from the former silent man of No. 10, Lord (Bernard) Donoghue, to whom I had written mostly out of interest in his recreation listed in *Who's Who* ('The Gay Hussar'). I still do not know whether this is an obscure board-game or a Scottish country dance, like the Gay Gordons. Mr Donoghue gets in the book for my second most brusque reply, writing across my letter to him: 'Not me. But try Joe Haines on the *Mirror*.' I took this to mean Mr Joe Haines on the *Mirror*, the infamous gamekeeper turned poacher (surely the wrong way round), I could not possibly try him.

Cruellest reply of all came from Mr Roy Jenkins, who wrote that he had not gone in for this sort of caper in thirty-eight years and did not intend to start now. I can see why he has so many friends in the Labour Party. Mr Gerald Kaufman wrote saying, sadly, he could not assist me: so if he feels hard done by at the vicious barbs directed against him he need look no further than his own book, *How to be a Minister*, page 177: 'It is your right to refuse talking to a journalist, though he may afterwards find ways of penalizing you.'

It would be ungracious not to express gratitude to other political journalists whom I have tried to be sparing in quoting but whose invective usually beats the politicians hands down. I would recommend all who have not done so to read the two portraits of life at Westminster by my colleague Mr Edward Pearce. Unlike other sketch writers' works, his *Senate of Lilliput* and *Hummingbirds and Hyenas* are not recycled old columns but new offerings. I had thought the same about *Empty Seats* by Michael White of *The Guardian* (clever title that, all those deserted benches) until, two-thirds through the book, I realized this was not Michael White of *The Guardian* but Michael White, impresario and confidant of Koo Stark. The book was sadly not about Westminster at all.

Hopefully, *The Official Candidate's Book of Political Insults* will fill a yawning gap in current political literature. It was deliberately decided to concentrate upon the Thatcher-Reagan years as modern material is so sadly lacking (a recent major publisher's definitive work on political quotations, for example, revealingly contained nothing by David Owen *or* David Steel).

For candidates, the chapter on how to deal with hecklers (14) and the A–Z of suggested insults to trip up foes should prove especially valuable. But all readers with an interest in politics should find something to savour in this at times vicious, at times rude, but always, I hope, witty, compendium.

Graham Jones,
Barnet,
Hertfordshire,
1987

1

Poodles, Polecats and a Clove of Garlic

He who allows himself to be insulted deserves to be.
Pierre Corneille (1606–84), Héraclius

The first thing all candidates must acknowledge is that the art of political insult is a delicate one. To be heavyhanded, to talk of 'guts left at Goose Green' as Mr Kinnock did in 1983, to boast 'we kicked a little ass last night' (Vice-President Bush after his TV debate with Mrs Geraldine Ferraro), or to call the Prime Minister 'a bounder, a liar, a deceiver, a cheat, a crook' (Mr Tam Dalyell), is to invite a deluge of bogus moral indignation and shouts of 'Own goal!'

Only a mighty High Lord can get away with 'muttering "bollocks" *sotto voce* to the Bishops', though an assiduously built reputation as a 'semi-housetrained polecat' (Michael Foot's attack assured Norman Tebbit's later eminence) can work wonders.

The well-struck needle in the groin can be most effective in drawing opponents' blood. (Mr Kinnock, with his penchant for doctor's waiting-room vernacular, was riled into describing Mr Tebbit's style as 'like a boil on a verruca' while Mr Healey feigned fending him off with a crucifix and a clove of garlic.)

For the novice, sharply-honed wit and a self-deprecating manner are the most productive.

Remember, 'Please don't applaud—it might annoy your neighbour', strategically said at the Tory Party Conference, all but achieved the impossible—the rehabilitation of Mr Edward Heath. Best to build on the tried and trusted: such as Edward Kennedy's description of Senator Fritz Hollings: 'The only non-English-speaking candidate ever to run for President;' or Tory MP Andrew MacKay on Mrs Edwina Currie: 'She has done as much for our party as King Herod did for baby sitting.'

Later the professional eye turns to a fifteen-second spot on the early evening news. With this in view it is fair to say that in the

1

Yuppie, Reagan-Thatcher (or should it be 'Saatchi and Saatchi') years the art of political insult has steadily moved to unrelinquished verbal brutality:

> To call the Prime Minister's speech 'crocodile tears with crocodile teeth', as Mr Kinnock did, is unfair on crocodiles.
> *Rodney Bickerstaffe, General Secretary of NUPE*

> How do we know that next time, as always in the past, when President Reagan says 'Jump', she will not reply 'How high?'
> *Denis Healey on Margaret Thatcher*

> The Prime Minister tells us that she has given the French President a piece of her mind—not a gift I would receive with alacrity.
> *Denis Healey*

Mrs Thatcher has been the most metaphor-bludgeoned Prime Minister since Chamberlain, even in success: a whole chapter on this blitzkrieg later. And as Edward Heath said on welcoming Mr Denis Thatcher to a Lord's Taverners lunch:

> I want to say how much we admire him.

Ronald Reagan has a nice line in studied insults. What is there new to call a rabid terrorist like Colonel Gaddafi? The US President managed it:

Not only a barbarian, but flaky.

While a senior aide had the ideal put-down for the smooth-talking Gorbachov team at the Reykjavik summit:

Blow-dried Bolsheviks.

In reverse, others have been just as unkind to the 'superannuated cowboy actor':

He has done for monetarism what the Boston Strangler did for door-to-door salesmen.

Denis Healey

He has achieved a breakthrough in political technology—the Teflon-coated Presidency. He sees to it that nothing sticks to him.
Congresswoman Pat Schroeder (An addendum from elsewhere was that by contrast George Bush was the Velcro Vice President—just about everything stuck to him.)

Political invective is now an international industry.

Q. What is 16 stone and still a lightweight?
A. David Lange, the Prime Minister of New Zealand.
Diplomatic community joke after his London press conference. ('Like a budgerigar trying to be a condor' observed Paul Callan, of the Daily Mirror.*)*

In fact, in Britain, Mrs Thatcher does have rivals for the title of 'most abused politician'.

I always think the East End sobriquet 'Big 'ead' fits David Owen better than anyone I know.

Ian Mikardo

I'm reminded of Dame Sybil Thorndike's comment on her long marriage. She considered: 'divorce, never, murder frequently.' With Dr Owen it is 'murder, occasionally'.

David Steel

Dr Owen does not shirk from wounding in return, however, calling Labour's Deputy Leader, Roy Hattersley, for example:

The acceptable face of opportunism.

. . . Mr Hattersley having made one of the most celebrated asides of the Saatchi and Saatchi years, whistling up to Darlington after his party's débâcle at Bermondsey and observing, according to Peter Tatchell;

Thank God there are no poofs in this by-election.

The issue of 'gay rights' had come to the forefront with the rise of the 'hard' Left, particularly in London, bringing this cartoon caption from JAK in the *Evening Standard*:

Eighty-six years ago Oscar Wilde got sent to prison for it, fourteen years ago it was made legal, and now under Ken Livingstone it's going to be compulsory!

Luminaries of the far Left came in for remorseless hammering from the popular press, such as this from columnist Jimmy Reid in the Maxwell-house-magazine, the *Daily Mirror*:

A butterfly Bolshie . . . a joke . . . Tony Benn has had more roads to Damascus than a Syrian long-distance lorry driver.

Michael Foot's career as Leader of the Labour Party was the first ended by verbal offence since Lansbury. He was called 'Worzel Gummidge' and 'Old Father Time', 'an elderly, ranting pamphleteer', though what really upset him was an attack by *The Economist* which jibed at his lack of knowledge of sociology and economics, said he had found being a Minister 'hard to master' and described his 'jaws rigid and lips flecked with spittle'.

Do not make the mistake of thinking there is no humour on the Left, however. On his first meeting with the then Transport Minister, Mr Norman Fowler, 'Red Ken' Livingstone emerged to say (in a reply to those cartoons?):

He asked to see me again. I think he wants me for my body.

In recent years the House of Commons has been somewhat eclipsed by ITN as the theatre of political thrust and counter-thrust, but still has its memorable moments. Labour front-bencher Peter Snape described Mr Richard Needham, once Jim Prior's PPS and subsequently Patrick Jenkin's, as:

A man who, having escaped from the Titanic, has clambered aboard the Marie Celeste.

4

(Yes, the order 'abandon ship', that one at least, came from No. 10 shortly afterwards.)

Mrs Thatcher does not always approach the dispatch box at Question Time with guns blazing. She can show a little humour too:

MR SYDNEY BIDWELL: Is the Rt Hon Lady aware that Mr Len Murray, the General Secretary of the TUC, insists that when he sees her, it is like having a dialogue with the deaf?
THE PRIME MINISTER: I had no idea that Mr Murray was deaf.

As can the razor-tongued Mr Norman Tebbit, here heard in a well-worth-recycling rebuke to Labour's Mr David Winnick:

If providence had not pre-empted him, the Hon Gentleman would be in danger of making a fool of himself.

To dole out such medicine, of course, requires a readiness to take it in return:

Putting Norman Tebbit in charge of industrial relations is like appointing Dracula to take charge of the blood transfusion service.
Shadow Employment Secretary Eric Varley

Ministers must develop hides like Sherman tanks. Leon Brittan, fluffing over the BBC's *Real Lives* documentary, was described by Lord Annan as behaving like:

A demented poodle.

While Lord Whitelaw's appointment to be in charge of preventing 'banana skins' was described by Gerald Kaufman as:

Like appointing Elizabeth Arden to make Ena Sharples look like Raquel Welch.

That is nothing compared with the verbal shearing Sir Geoffrey Howe has been forced to endure. Julia Langdon in the *Daily Mirror* reported how one Cabinet Minister had said of the soft-spoken Foreign Secretary:

I know now when he is speaking—I can see his lips moving.

One also sympathises with the teachers' bogeyman, Sir Keith Joseph, described by Simon Hoggart in his book *On the House* as:

Like Woody Allen without the jokes.

The bright, ambitious and terrier-like Mrs Edwina Currie faced a cruel campaign of jealous male disapprobation: she was told by Labour's Frank Dobson:

When you go to the dentist, he's the one who must need the anaesthetic.

Another MP quoted by *The Tatler* observed:

She is writing a book. It is called *Famous People Who Have Met Me*.

But Mrs Currie, who sparked one of the most fearsome insult-hurling contests of recent years when she said Mr Kinnock was ruled by the person who made him breakfast, was clearly on the up, one of the unexpected political success stories of the Reagan-Thatcher years. Another was Hollywood star Clint Eastwood, who exchanged his horse, cigarillo and man-with-no-name tag to become mayor of Carmel-by-the-Sea, California.

Ronald Reagan's response was the ideal political jibe for all candidates to aim at: witty, to the point, and with a streak of self-deprecation. Making the obligatory call of congratulation, the President (star of *Bedtime for Bonzo*) inquired of Mr Eastwood (star of *Every Which Way but Loose*):

What's an actor who's played in a movie with a monkey doing in politics?

2

Party Political Broadsides

They are nothing else but a load of kippers—two faced, with no guts.
Eric Heffer on the Tories

I don't belong to any organized party—I'm Labour.
Voter quoted by Austin Mitchell

They're like a bunch of bananas—green round the edges, soft in the middle, and not quite straight.
Michael Heseltine on the SDP

Pluralist politics naturally brings a collective breed of insult—you might call it the party political broadside. There may be a problem of whom to attack for maximum effect. But party pickings come thick, fast, and without mercy.

Conservatives

They travel best in gangs, hanging around like bunches of bananas—thick-skinned and yellow.
Neil Kinnock (with yet another slur on this poor defenceless fruit)

The cream of Britain—rich, thick and full of clots.
Car sticker

Tories are always wrong—but they are always wrong at the right moment.
Lady Violet Bonham-Carter

The only thing wrong with the Tory Party is the people who are in it.
John Lydon

SNOB!

SLOB!

Labour

One of the most damning indictments of the Labour Party, at least in the first years of the Thatcher reign, came from a surprising source—its own MP for Grimsby, Mr Austin Mitchell, in a book entitled *Four Years in the Death of the Labour Party.* 'The prickly party,' he called it. 'The Red Titanic . . . on a ski slope to disaster.'

Of the 1983 election he said: 'Labour was as well prepared as Poland in September 1939.' Labour's programme in 1982 he called:

A guide to Bennite Britain . . . not so much a labour of love as a premature ejaculation.

Going on to warn:

Recirculated sewage is still sewage.

Others have been equally unkind:

Labour is the party of verbal elastoplast and they can't even stitch up their divisions.

David Owen

The difference between the extremists and the moderates in the Labour Party is that the extremists want to abolish private education now, the moderates want to wait until their own children have finished school.

Nigel Lawson

8

The voters are not daft. They can smell a rat whether it is wrapped in a red flag or covered in roses.

Norman Tebbit

Labour's problem is that it is a doctrinal party without a doctrine.

Tom Ellis

I don't often attack the Labour Party—they do it so well themselves.

Edward Heath

Liberals

CSCs—conscience-stricken capitalists.

Lord Jenkins of Putney

Poujadists.

Ron Brown (Leith)

Dr Barnardo's home for orphan voters.

Quoted by Gerry Neale, MP

The Muddled Tendency.

Margaret Thatcher

You can always tell a Young Liberal in any crowd. He will be the one being chased by a red-faced Liberal Party official as he hops along, one foot clenched firmly in his mouth.

Editorial in the Social Democrat

If God had been a Liberal, there wouldn't have been Ten Commandments—just ten suggestions.

Malcolm Bradbury and Christopher Brigby, TV play After Dinner Game, *quoted in* The Penguin Dictionary of Modern Quotations

Scottish Nationalists

Tartan terrors.

George Foulkes

Political maggots.

Dennis Canavan

The Wilson/Stewart duo without music.

Ron Brown (Leith)

Democratic Unionist Party

The God, Showbiz, and Related Trades Party.

Austin Mitchell

Social Democrats

It is hardly surprising that as a new party, initially at least posing a threat to the established order, the SDP should be showered with a torrent of abuse. That isn't to say that some of the epithets haven't been the height of invention or humour . . .

The soggies. *Liberal diehards*

The bland leading the bland. *Walter Terry*, The Sun

SDP = Socialist Defectors Party. *Lord Jenkins of Putney*

The socialite party. *Ron Brown (Leith)*

Social Demo-rats. *Ron Hayward*

Trying to build a land fit for credit-card holders.

Roy Hattersley

Political lounge lizards. *Neil Kinnock*

Policies like liquid grease. *Neil Kinnock*

The heterosexual wing of the Liberal Party. *George Foulkes*

The world's most boring party. They were born yawning.

Jon Akass

The SDP should have been strangled at birth. *Cyril Smith*

3

State of the Art

The self-appointed king of the gutter.
Michael Heseltine on Neil Kinnock after his 'guts at Goose Green' attack,
1983 election

If I was in the gutter, and I ain't, he'd still be looking up at me from the
sewer.
Neil Kinnock on Michael Heseltine, in reply

All impartial observers are agreed: like nostalgia, political invective just 'ain't' what it used to be. They are not exactly agreed,
however, on why. Certainly the days of the great parliamentary
orators have passed, and with them, those of the silken slur
delivered with precision and wit in velvet glove: 'Begotten by
froth out of foam' (Asquith on Churchill); 'Smile like a silver plate
on a coffin,' (Daniel O'Connell on Peel); 'Forever poised between
a cliché and an indiscretion,' (Macmillan on Eden).

Giving notice of resigning his seat for the coming election, John
Watson, Conservative MP for Skipton and Ripon, cited as one
reason the noticeable falling in standards of parliamentary
behaviour.

Debates are frequently ill-attended by MPs. Their speeches are
frequently ill-attended by knowledge or logic. Historically the
Chamber was enriched by genuine wit and debating skill.
Today such niceties are all too often submerged beneath
raucous abuse.

It was a point also made by Nicholas Fairbairn, himself possess-
ing something of a bottomless cupboard of wit plus a wardrobe to
match. 'I am sorry to say that a sense of humour today is a
drawback,' says the former Scottish Solicitor-General. 'Had I
never had a sense of humour, I undoubtedly would be in the
Cabinet.'

11

Mr Fairbairn's view is that MPs have lost not only their love of language but their humanity. The old Lairds of the Tory Party had to know all their employees inside out to make their estates work. Working-class Labour politicians like Ernest Bevin, who had actually seen life down a coal-mine, understood fully what human suffering was about. 'They had wit,' says Mr Fairbairn, 'because wit is the expression of human sensitivity. Today MPs on our side are mostly "consultants", and on the other side they are "sociologists", "lecturers" or "trade union officials". They are third-hand human beings out of touch with life. Yet life is wit—a subtle understanding of human triumph and tragedy.'

The world over, 'parliamentary exchanges' today are often verbal, or even physical, brawls. In December 1985, eight Labour Euro-MPs scuffled with a Tory MEP, Mr Paul Howell, under a Christmas tree in Strasbourg. Mr Howell was wrestled to the ground, punched and kicked after accusing the Labour MPs, who were making an unauthorized Christmas collection, of diverting the money to the Militant-run Liverpool City Council.

Scenes in the House of Commons can be loutish: there was, for example, the strange sight, in July 1986, of Mr Neil Kinnock making a Nazi salute and, according to Tory right-winger Nicholas Winterton, shouting 'Fascist' at him. He also was said to have hissed, in a reference to Mr Winterton's defence of South Africa: 'Boyo, you get paid.'

Shortly after Valentine's Day 1987 came the celebrated Sir Marcus Fox motion on Mr Kinnock (withdrawn), and labelled by the avenging hero of Indian restaurant skirmishes 'slippage from the gutter into the sewer'.

Certainly the political leaders of today, much judged by their peers (in the non-parliamentary sense) on how they come across on television, have little of the linguistic elegance of their forebears. 'You f***er,' said Denis Healey to Dennis Canavan. 'Get lost,' says Mr Eric Heffer to just about everybody. Purists can also despair at the metaphors used by parliamentarians, typically wretched being Shadow Employment Secretary John Prescott's attack, in March 1986, on a speech by Kenneth Clarke as 'too long with no jobs in it, like a six-foot spotted dick with no spots'.

At recent elections we have seen scurrilous leaflets from the Liberals hinting at marital aberrations of other candidates; the incisive remark from Mrs Edwina Currie that the Liberal at West Derbyshire was 'a pompous prat'; and the gentle humour of Mr Ken Livingstone's propaganda sheet, London Labour Briefing: 'What do you call four dead Tories? A start.'

The decline of political eloquence can be traced first to society's increased acceptance of obscenity (which previously would never have made newspaper or TV screen) as a substitute for genuine wit. Also, the broadcasters' thirst for quick-fire, blood-and-guts quotes and exchanges (the bloodier, the 'better television') has emasculated the blow from the silver cutlass.

Whither Political Invective?

Just as Mr Rupert Murdoch was ahead of his time in Australia with what became the down-market British and American tabloids of today, it is perhaps to the Antipodes we should look to assess the likely style of political invective tomorrow.

The extraordinary accession of Bob Hawke to the premiership of Australia in 1983 sets the scene. Former Labour Leader Bill Hayden was pushed aside with all the subtlety of mutton corralled for a sheep dip, while protesting: 'I can't stand down for a bastard like Bob Hawke.' This last stand was promptly repulsed by the acting Brutus, Senator Button, who replied: 'In my experience in the Labour Party, the fact that someone is a bastard (of one kind or another) has never been a disqualification for leadership.'

It is what you might call politics retreating to the lager—for plainly no one gives an XXXX for any opponent's sensibilities.

Last year, according to *Daily Star* diarist Peter Tory, the down-under insult champ was Federal Treasurer Paul Keating MP who notched up in parliament: harlot, cheat, pig, mug, boxhead, clot, fop, sucker, thug, piece of criminal garbage, gutless spiv and (wait for it) . . . sleazebag.

New Zealand politics produces the same natty line in political vernacular. The prime minister, former Methodist lay-preacher David Lange, has hit out at the 'cringers and whingers' and told striking teachers at a kindergarten party: 'I think you should piss off.'

America, too, has a tradition of expletives deleted, and David Stockman in his recent autobiography told how he received a lesson in vituperative admonishment from the then White House Chief of Staff, James Baker:

My friend, I want you to listen up good. Your ass is in a sling. All the rest of them want you shit-canned right now. If it weren't for me you'd be a goner already. But I got you one last chance to save yourself. You're going to have lunch with the President. The menu is humble pie. You're going to eat every last f***ing spoonful of it. You're going to be the most contrite sonofabitch this world has ever seen. When you go through the Oval Office door, I want to see that sorry ass of yours dragging on the carpet.

Americans have stretched the level of political raillery to the very limits of the English language. Columnist and modern idiom guru William Safire worked for Spiro Agnew and came up with 'pusillanimous pussyfooters' and 'nattering nabobs of nega-tivism'. Senator Fritz Hollings called David Stockman 'a patho-logical finangler' and fired off an unforgettable salvo to the opposition over the MX missile: 'Dense pack is an appropriate name for more than just a missile configuration.'

In the British Parliament gentlemanly ribbing is encouraged by strict ground rules that forbid the direct accusation by licensing talk only in the third person: 'The Rt Hon Gentleman said . . .' and so on. Accusations of lying, dishonesty or drunkenness are strictly out of order, unless put 'hypothetically', and thus the favourite insults are 'hypocrisy', 'fatuous deception' and 'crawling to the Americans/South Africans/Soviets/financiers/council-house tenants', etc.

That is not to say the determined, like Mr Andrew Faulds, are deterred from shouting 'slime, Fascist, Pharisee, she picked you out of the gutter' to the likes of Mr Norman Tebbit. But the encouragement is always there to true wit. Mrs Thatcher's 'cuckoo' remarks about the Bishops in March 1985 brought the predictable question from Mr Derek Fatchett (Lab, Leeds Central) who asked what other bird species troubled the divided Conservative Party. 'None,' replied Mrs Thatcher sweetly, clearly seeding out Mr Edward Heath for a coded mention: 'Apart, that is, from the odd grouse.'

Internal Labour Party fraternal greetings are, of course, seldom as fraternal as this, as in the celebrated exchange from July 1983 after the party Leader, Mr Michael Foot, refused to back discussion of changes to the block vote system of electing his successor:

ROY HATTERSLEY: You have betrayed us. What kind of leadership is this?
MICHAEL FOOT: Don't talk to me like that. I'll have your head off. I'll have the skin off your back.
ROY HATTERSLEY: You couldn't knock the skin off a rice pudding.

The man who eventually did succeed Mr Foot, Neil Kinnock, has a turgid and treacly verbal style, with a tendency to depart from his crisp, prepared text and pile on the subsidiary clauses with a shovel. As at Glamorgan at the end of the last election campaign:

If Margaret Thatcher wins on Thursday, she will be more a leader than a Prime Minister. That power produces arrogance and when it is toughened by Tebbitry and flattened and fawned upon by spineless sycophants, the boot-licking tabloid knights of Fleet Street and placemen in the quangos, the arrogance corrupts absolutely.

Perhaps it should be mentioned in his defence that Mr Kinnock's repertoire is far wider than mere prose. Addressing a Labour Party rally at Brecon, North Wales in July 1985, he gleefully broke into verse to ridicule Mr Nicholas Ridley's collapsed plans for privatizing water authorities:

The boy stood on the burning deck,
His time was getting shorter,
His plans were wrapped around his neck,
He could not privatize water.

Mr Kinnock's occasionally pugilistic style has its precursors, of course. Even ignoring Mr Heseltine's swinging of the mace above his head, there was the celebrated Derbyshire mining MP, Tom

Swain, who shouted to a Tory: 'Say that outside and I'll punch your bloody head in.' (This was, said one journalist, his best and most articulate speech in seventeen years in the House.) In May 1985, Welsh Nationalist Dafydd Wigley broke off part of the Speaker's chair. Emanuel Shinwell and Bernadette Devlin both crossed the floor to slap Conservatives in the face, and a fellow Labour MP once scuffled with Neil Kinnock.

On the increase it certainly is, but it would be folly to suggest parliamentary hooliganism is purely a modern-day phenomenon. The very lay-out of the chamber, with two swords' lengths between Government and Opposition front benches, was a response to the possibility of murder on the premises even if carried out under gentlemen's terms of chivalry.

Mere words, of course, may not be enough to win a political argument, particularly when it comes to tough international summits or industrial bargaining. Many union leaders have adopted the traditional tactic for wearing the opposition down, i.e. interminable repetition in a low flat voice. (Two variants being the current TUC General Secretary Mr Norman Willis's excruciating jokes and Sir Harold Wilson's answer to insulting Commonwealth conference harangues—puffing a large pipeful of tobacco until they wore themselves out.)

In the Commons, Dennis Skinner is noted for his ability to create a diversionary verbal punch-up to distract opponents, though one of the neatest tricks came from Michael Foot who astonished the Conservative benches by demanding that all who supported current Government policies should put up their hands. Six hesitant palms reached upwards, to hoots of derision from the Labour side.

There is also the 'rough diamond' approach, what is known in the well-hackneyed phrase as 'calling a spade a bloody shovel'. In recent years the prime master of blunt talk has been Liberal MP Cyril Smith. He was the man who, after the celebrated court case, delighted Jeremy Thorpe with: 'Shot any dogs lately?' He said of the SDP Leader William Rodgers, in a dispute about the allocation of Alliance seats: 'He's acting like an overgrown schoolgirl . . . he's poncing about the stage like a prima donna.' And his abortive deputy leadership bid brought a message to fellow Liberals: 'You can get stuffed.'

But here is a true believer in old-fashioned larger-than-Cyril parliamentary style and wit: 'Pitt, Disraeli and Gladstone fired the House of Commons with life,' the Rochdale MP wrote in his autobiography. 'The present incumbents, it seems to me, are capable only of the kiss of death.' The great days of political invective, RIP.

16

4

The Professionals' Choice: Great Ripostes

Professional politicians were asked to nominate their favourite ripostes, put-downs and taunts to the troublesome:

PETER ARCHER, QC, MP,
Warley West
Labour's Shadow Northern Ireland Secretary

MAN IN CROWD: Christianity has been on the earth for 2,000 years, and look at the state of the world today.
DONALD (NOW LORD) SOPER: Water has been on the earth longer than that, and look at the colour of your neck.

LORD BROCKWAY (LAB),
long-standing parliamentarian and pacifist

The most amusing retorts I have come across were by a well-known Hyde Park Speakers' Corner orator named Adolf Kohn.

I'LL SWAP YOU HALF-A-DOZEN GRATUITOUS INSULTS FOR FOUR BARBED RIPOSTES

COMMUNIST HECKLER: Do you agree that political parties are the expression of the interest of sections of classes?
ADOLF KOHN: Yes.
HECKLER: In that case, Mr Speaker, which section of the capitalist classes does the Communist Party represent?
KOHN: The undertakers.

HECKLER: Tell us when this 'ere revolution is going to happen.
KOHN: Next Thursday afternoon, 2.30. Leave your address and we'll send you a postcard.

SYDNEY CHAPMAN, MP,
Chipping Barnet (C)

When I inaugurated 'Plant-a-Tree Year' in 1973 I was also Hon Secretary of the Animal Welfare Parliamentary Group. When I entered the Members' smoking-room shortly afterwards I was greeted by an orchestrated chorus of 'How's the Doggie's Delight tonight?'

EDWINA CURRIE, MP,
Derbyshire South (C)
The Conservatives' junior Health Minister

This is my own version of a story told by Lord Denning at his retirement dinner and explains why women can't be politicians.

'Please do remember this: if a politician says "yes", then he means "maybe". If he says "maybe", he means "no". And if he says "no", then he's not a politician.

'But if a lady says "no", she means "maybe". And if she says "maybe", she means "yes". And if she says "yes", then she's not a lady.

'That is why politics and women don't mix.'

JOHN EDMONDS
General Secretary of the General Municipal
Boilermakers and Allied Trades Union

RODNEY BICKERSTAFFE OF NUPE, on a Thatcher Cabinet re-shuffle: Change—it's like being cured of a diarrhoea and then finding that you have dysentery.

MICK MCGAHEY, after listening to an enthusiast talking about wind power and alternative energy sources: I don't think that I will spend much time tilting at windmills.

TOM ELLIS
SDP candidate for Clwyd South West,
former MP for Wrexham

'Strong jawed and jelly minded.' Description of Barry Jones, recently Shadow Welsh Secretary, in a letter in the *Liverpool Daily Post.*

'That Robespierre of the raspberries.' Description of Gwynfor Evans, former President of Plaid Cymru and MP for Carmarthen, given by Wynford Vaughan Thomas in a moment of exasperation. Gwynfor was a market gardener at the time.

NICHOLAS FAIRBAIRN, MP,
Perth and Kinross (C)

While Foreign Secretary Sir Alec Douglas-Home visited China and was sitting next to Chairman Mao. Alec said: 'Tell me, Mr Chairman, what do you think would have happened if Mr Khrushchev had been assassinated and not President Kennedy?' Chairman Mao paused for a moment, then replied drily: 'I do not believe Mr Onassis would have married Mrs Khrushchev.'

EARL FERRERS (C),
former Minister of State for Agriculture
and Deputy Leader of the House of Lords

LORD CARRINGTON, to Lord Longford, when Leader of the House: The Noble Lord Longford is getting angry—and when he gets angry, he is usually wrong.

When I gave an evasive reply to a supplementary question (because I did not know the answer) Baroness Summerskill gave a withering riposte: 'The Noble Lord really must do his homework. Everyone knows that that has been the situation, ever since the Noble Lord was a little boy.'
 I replied (it was all I could think of): 'A lot of things happened when I was a little boy of which the Noble Baroness would be a great deal more aware of than me.'

MICHAEL FOOT, MP,
Ebbw Vale (Lab),
former Leader of the Labour Party

From the *Daily Telegraph* of June 1986 (sketch written by

Edward Pearce): 'Mr Foot makes up for not believing in God by looking rather like him.'

GEORGE FOULKES, MP,
Carrick, Cumnock and Doon Valley (Lab)

Bill Walker (Conservative, North Tayside) pompous as usual, droned on about the Labour Opposition having no grounds for criticizing the Government's economic record, recalling the time when Denis Healey was Chancellor and he had to call on the assistance of the IMF.

Piped up an irreverent Labour heckler: 'Come off it Bill. Up until then you thought the IMF was a cheap furniture store.'

JOHN GOLDING
General Secretary, National Communications Union,
former MP for Newcastle under Lyme (Lab)

I once rose to interrupt a front-bench spokesman, on our side, who was also a barrister and used to spend a lot of his time in court. He protested: would the Hon Gentleman kindly not interrupt him in the middle of his sentence.

I said: 'Oh, I was under the impression that it was generally the Rt Hon Gentleman's clients who were in the middle of their sentences.'

SIR ELDON GRIFFITHS, MP,
Bury St Edmunds (C)

Stanley Orme was asked by Sally Oppenheim how the Right Honourable Gentleman would explain the point he was making, if he were Minister for Consumer Affairs, to 'the man on the shop floor'. Orme's riposte in ripe Northern tongue: 'The only shop floor the Right Honourable Lady knows anything about is the shop floor of Fortnum and Mason's.'

My description of Harold Wilson: 'He displays all the political morals of an alley-cat.'

ILLTYD HARRINGTON
former Deputy Leader of the GLC

My own words to Harvey Hinds, a former Canon of the Church of England and Chief Whip of the Labour Party at the GLC were: 'Your bloody trouble is you escaped from a novel by Trollope and you can't find your way back into the cloister.'

I once told Harold Wilson: 'Your basic trouble is your eyes look in.'

JERRY HAYES, MP,
Harlow (C)

GERALD KAUFMAN, on Nicholas Edwards: He knows little about most things and absolutely nothing about everything else.

NORMAN TEBBIT, to Dennis Skinner: Far better to keep your mouth shut and let everyone think you're stupid than to open it and leave no doubt.

JOHN MCWILLIAM, MP,
Blaydon (Lab)

'Will the Rt Hon Gentleman tell the House what future generations have ever done for him?' (Rt Hon J. E. Powell interrupting Norman Fowler when he was announcing a large increase in gas prices.)

STEPHEN ROSS, MP,
Isle of Wight (Lib)

REV T. W. MCCREA (DUP), about Mrs Thatcher on the Anglo-Irish Agreement: How could she take that viper to suckle at her breast?
CLEMENT FREUD, to John Hume (SDLP) in a private note: No self-respecting viper would suckle at that breast!

CYRIL SMITH, to Arthur Lewis, MP: Sit down, shrimp!

o

DAVID STEEL, MP,
Tweedale, Etterick and Lauderdale
Leader of the Liberal Party

I have used this reply to good effect on a number of occasions: 'Of course I don't disagree with everything you say. Even a broken clock is right twice a day.'

My favourite piece of invective came to my mind while visiting Cruft's: 'Mrs Thatcher has turned the British bulldog into President Reagan's poodle.'

DAVID TRIPPIER, MP,
Rossendale and Darwen (C)
the Conservatives' junior Employment Minister

Reply by myself to Dennis Skinner, MP: 'On this subject the Hon Gentleman suffers from delusions of adequacy.'

JOHN WATSON, MP,
Skipton and Ripon (C)

When Roy Jenkins resigned from the House of Commons in order to take up a lucrative job in Europe, the Labour MP for Ashfield, David Marquand, resigned at the same time, also to go to Europe. (For the purposes of this tale, it is necessary to remember both that David Marquand was never a particularly popular MP in the House of Commons and also that Roy Jenkins tends to pronounce his Rs as Ws.) As Mr Jenkins came to the end of his farewell speech he said: 'I want you to know that I leave this great chamber without rancour.' At which one rough Yorkshire voice from behind him shouted: 'I thought you were taking him with you.'

5

Two All-time Greats

Theodore Roosevelt

The self-proclaimed 'bull moose', who became US President in 1901 on the assassination of William McKinley, was a giant of a politician, the all-American favourite who combined a rugged Sylvester Stallone frame with a deep intellect. He may have headed the legendary 'Rough Riders' and climbed trees for relaxation but he was a *magna cum laude* graduate at Harvard, lectured at Oxford and the Sorbonne, read three books a day and learnedly wrote 18 million words.

He was also America's all-time giant of political invective, a man who enjoyed the biting phrase purely for the intellectual satisfaction of it. He loved the fun of hating, betrayed by the fact that when he delivered a polished gem, said Booth Tarkington, you could hear 'an undertone of Homeric chuckling'.

'Teddy' endowed twentieth-century political language with a rich legacy: 'hyphenated Americans', 'weasel words', 'the right stuff', 'the lunatic fringe' and 'the mollycoddle vote'. He brought us such phrases as: 'the millennium is quite a long way off yet', 'speak softly and carry a big stick', 'stagnation has continued with uninterrupted violence' and 'hardness of heart does nothing like as much harm as softness of head'. And the well-honed words he thrust at opponents would leave any modern politician standing.

Among his great insults he called President Marroquin of Columbia 'a pithecanthropoid' (= half man, half ape), President Castro of Venezuela 'an unspeakably villainous little monkey', Senator William Alfred Peffer 'a well-meaning, pin-headed, anarchistic crank, of hirsute and slabsided aspect', and one New York Supreme Court Justice 'an amiable old fuzzy-wuzzy with sweetbread brains'.

President McKinley, whom he succeeded, had 'about as much backbone as a chocolate eclair', while he characterized his successor, Woodrow Wilson, as 'a Byzantine logothete'.

Meanwhile, George Bernard Shaw was a 'blue-rumped ape',

Sir Mortimer Durand, British Ambassador to Washington, 'a fellow with a mind which functions at six guinea-pig power'. Critics of his Panama policy were 'a small bunch of shrill eunuchs', demonstrators against bloodsports 'logical vegetarians of the flabbiest Hindoo type', while Jefferson Davis enjoyed 'the unique distinction of being the only American with whose public character Benedict Arnold need not fear comparison'.

Roosevelt was also adept at political abuse from the platform. Following William Jennings Bryan at the Chicago Coliseum, he declared: 'It is not merely schoolgirls who have hysterics; very vicious mob leaders have them at times, and so do well-meaning demagogues when their minds are turned by the applause of men of little intelligence.' Bryan, he said: '. . . represents only that type of farmer whose gate hangs on one hinge, whose old hat supplies the place of the missing window pane, and who is more likely to be found at the cross-roads grocery store than behind the plough.'

Hecklers were dispatched with relish. When one, referring to alleged malpractice in food supplies by the government during the Spanish war, cried out 'What about the rotten beef?' Roosevelt snorted back with venom: 'I ate it and you'll never get near enough to be hit by a bullet or within five miles of it.' This remark caused a riot.

Perhaps the most penetrating sallies came against members of the Populist Party, and here he employed his full elegance of language. 'That a man should change his clothes in the evening, that he should dine at any hour other than noon, impress these good people as being symptoms of depravity instead of merely trivial,' he said. 'A taste for learning and cultivated friends, and a tendency to bathe frequently, cause in them the deepest suspicion.'

Certainly no one could accuse Roosevelt of 'pussyfooting'. You guessed—that most famous of insults was one of his, too.

Benjamin Disraeli

Twice British Tory Prime Minister, Benjamin Disraeli (1804–81) is without doubt to political insult what Mozart is to music or Rembrandt to portraiture, giving us such gems as 'he has to learn that petulance is not sarcasm and insolence is not invective'; 'he played upon the House of Commons like an Old Fiddle'; and 'he is a self-made man, and worships his creator'.

'Dizzy's' resonant literary style was in part due to his career as a novelist (he had published his first work, *Vivian Gray*, at the age of twenty-two), and a daring, cavalier approach to his opponents was to give him the edge in debate over his arch-rival, Gladstone. It was of Gladstone that he said 'If he fell into the Thames, that would be a misfortune, and if anyone pulled him out, that I suppose would be a calamity', sketching him as 'a sophisticated rhetorician, inebriated with the exuberance of his own verbosity, and gifted with an egotistical imagination that can at all times command an interminable and inconsistent series of arguments to malign an opponent and to glorify himself.'

In one heated debate, Gladstone shouted at him: 'Mr Disraeli cannot be sure of his facts.' 'I wish,' said Disraeli, 'that I could be as sure of anything as my opponent is of everything.' On another occasion he said of Gladstone: 'He has not a single redeeming defect.'

Another enemy was Gladstone's fellow Liberal, Lord John Russell. In Disraeli's opinion: 'If a traveller were informed that such a man was Leader of the House of Commons, he might begin to comprehend how the Egyptians worshipped an insect.'

Many of his famous 'off the cuff' ripostes were in fact scripted well in advance. What made him excel, like any master of humour, was his timing. It was said Gladstone could immediately tell when a *bon mot* was on its way by Disraeli's habit of putting a handkerchief to his mouth, signalling the pause that would make way for the witticism.

But Disraeli remains an inspiration to all prospective politicians and many have recirculated his jibes. Peel, whom he destroyed, he accused of 'catching the Whigs bathing, and walking away with their clothes'; of being 'a burglar of other intellects . . . there is no statesman who has committed political larceny on so grand a scale.' Palmerston was dispatched as: 'That great Apollo of aspiring undertrappers, menacing Russia with a perfumed cane.' Lord Liverpool: 'The arch-mediocrity who presided, rather than ruled, over a cabinet of mediocrities . . . not a statesman, a statemonger . . . peremptory in little questions, the great ones are left open.'

Other opponents were mocked as 'that weird Sybil', 'looking and speaking like a cheesemonger' and 'like an old goat on Mount Haemus'. When someone talked of an MP being 'out of his depth', Disraeli said: 'Out of his depth? Why, he's three miles from shore!'

His humble origins had helped sharpen his wit, which he often used to defend himself. When an enemy remarked that his wife had picked him out of the gutter, Disraeli countered with: 'My good fellow, if you were in the gutter, no one would pick *you* out.'

In defence of his Jewish faith against another foe, Daniel O'Connell, Disraeli responded lyrically with: 'Yes, I am a Jew, and when the ancestors of the Rt Hon Gentleman were brutal savages in an unknown island, mine were priests in the temple of Solomon.'

Nevertheless, it is worth recording that not all Disraeli's utterances were sparkling and caused rolling in the aisles. According to his biographer, Lord Blake, when Disraeli attempted to make jokes about 'productivity' linked to women's pregnancy: 'Some of his remarks went too far for the taste of the House.'

6

Poison Portraits

Meeting David Mellor is like being hit in the face with a mouthful of Brylcreem.

John Edmonds, GMBATU General Secretary

The pen being mightier than the sword and the tongue usually being sharper than either, all politicians have at some stage been subjected to a rapier thrust. Among the best barbs:

Cabinet Table

VISCOUNT WHITELAW

Almost all he does turns into farce, fiasco and failure . . . One of the last representatives of a dying Tory tradition, possession of land, enthusiasm for shooting small birds and antipathy for reading books.

Roy Hattersley

NIGEL LAWSON

The Tory Party is split into two factions over Nigel Lawson: those who hate him, and those who loathe him.

Westminster joke quoted in The Observer

He could be bundled into a political dustbin without a squeak of protest from the voters, the City or even the Conservative Party. He is not a Chancellor. He is a manikin with a thick coating of bombast.

Roy Jenkins

PETER WALKER

To hear him talk, he has done almost as much for agriculture as fertilizer.

Frank Johnson

KENNETH BAKER

I should have thought it difficult for anyone to be sillier than Sir Keith Joseph: but Mr Baker has managed it.

Alan Watkins, The Observer

JOHN MOORE

His delivery at the dispatch box has all the bite of a rubber duck.

Marcia, Lady Falkender

JOHN BIFFEN

. . . is becoming to the Tories what the Ancient Mariner is to sea cruises.

Marcia, Lady Falkender, Mail on Sunday

NICHOLAS RIDLEY

One Tory said his appointment was the worst since a Roman Emperor made his horse a senator. Which is a trifle unfair . . . on Caligula's horse.

Chris Buckland, Sunday People

God Bless America

GEORGE BUSH

If Jeane Kirkpatrick were his running mate, at least there'd be some macho on the ticket.

1984 Washington joke

ALAN CRANSTON

Comes over on television with all the personality of a cauliflower.

Dermot Purgavie, Daily Mail

Trouble with Cranston supporting a freeze is that all the people of Alabama think it's a dessert.

Senator Fritz Hollings

THOMAS ENDERS

I finally met a man more arrogant than I.

Henry Kissinger

GERALDINE FERRARO

My husband and I have no intention of hiding our wealth—not like that four-million-dollar—I can't say it, but it rhymes with 'rich'.

Barbara Bush, 1984

TIP O'NEILL

A Hogarthian embodiment of the superstate he had laboured so long to maintain.

David Stockman

NANCY REAGAN

Nancy has this recurring nightmare: she's kidnapped, taken to A & S, and forced to buy dresses right off the rack.

Joey Adams

JOHN WARNER

Looks like Virginia has just elected the three biggest boobs in the country.

Said on his election to the Senate while courting Elizabeth Taylor

Labour Front Bench

ROY HATTERSLEY

The grand old man of the main chance.

Tory MP quoted by the Sunday Times

There are lies, damned lies, and Roy Hattersley.

Prof. John Vincent, The Sun

DENIS HEALEY

Mr Healey is one of the most insensitive know-alls in the history of politics. He has shot his party in the foot, and I think he will be carried off the field pretty soon.

Roy Jenkins

One feels that if he were ill, the PLP would agree to send a get-well card by 154 votes to 127 with 28 abstentions.

Simon Hoggart, On the House

GERALD KAUFMAN

Reminds me of our Jack Russell, William, who barks ferociously at everything and nothing.

Colin Welch, Daily Mail

MICHAEL MEACHER

He just cannot be allowed to go on rushing round like a demented Santa Claus, scattering imaginary tenners from his sleigh.

Neil Kinnock quoted by 'Crossbencher,' Sunday Express

PETER SNAPE

Like a well-known mint, he has a very firm exterior, but there is an awful lot of air in the middle.

Lynda Chalker

International

GISCARD D'ESTAING

He suffers from an inexplicable misfortune—unpopularity.

Paris left daily, Liberation

CHARLES HAUGHEY

The man who dug the hole for the country's descent to Third World status.

Peter Paterson, Daily Mail

BOB HAWKE

The former grog-artist, womanizer and Rhodes scholar has made himself in his first year the most unpopular Australian since Pharlap, the freak wonder horse of the 1930s.

The Observer

From under his cockatoo hairdo, the platitudes he has got by heart.

Patrick White, Nobel prizewinning author

DAVID LANGE

A clown and a buffoon.

Sir Robert Muldoon

FRANÇOIS MITTERRAND

His programme is enough to make Tony Benn's eyes pop out with envy. By rights he ought to be stuffed and put in a museum.

Paul Johnson

On the Back Benches

PADDY ASHDOWN

As it turned out, his speech probably did swing sufficient votes to beat the platform. The only trouble was that he was speaking for the other side.

Ian Aitken, The Guardian

TERRY DICKS

A sort of Arthur Mullard without the charm.

Edward Pearce, Daily Telegraph

AUSTIN MITCHELL

Trendy Austin Mitchell ('Aren't I funny?'—'No, you're not.').

Walter Terry, The Sun

Currently world record-holder for prolonged adolescence.
London Standard, *quoted by Andrew Roth*

Loose Alliance

They have a new colour. They call it Gold. It looks yellow to
me.
Margaret Thatcher

ROY JENKINS

If he had ever formed a government it would, if based on the
Prime Minister's personal acquaintance with his Ministers,
have been unusually compact, since he very rarely spoke to
anyone whom he did not know well, and this group was
severely limited in size.
Gerald Kaufman, How to be a Minister

A beached whale asleep on alien shores in the tidal wave of
David Owen's personal ambitions.
Larry Whitty

DAVID OWEN

John Stuart Mill rewritten by Ernest Hemingway.
Chris Patten

DAVID STEEL

He's always reminded me of his 'Spitting Image' as Ferret Face
. . . desperately trying to bite off someone he'll never be able to
chew.
Jean Rook, Daily Express

SHIRLEY WILLIAMS

How dare Shirley Williams blame her 'notorious reputation for
always being late and in a hurry' on the fact that she's a woman

and therefore has no wife? Having a full-time job is not an excuse for inefficiency.

Shirley Conran

Temporarily Out to Grass

JEFFREY ARCHER

Often speaks like a one-dimensional character who has sprung into the world from an airport bookstall . . . Sometimes, people who meet him for the first time can hardly believe it: they wonder if they have been the victims of a practical joke.

James Naughtie, The Guardian

TONY BENN

Did more harm to British industry in one speech than the combined efforts of the Luftwaffe and the U-boats did in the whole of the last war.

Cyril Smith

. . . tomfool issues . . . barmy ideas . . . a kind of ageing, perennial tough who immatures with age.

Harold Wilson

LEON BRITTAN

Looked like a bloke in the sixth form who never had a date.

Simon Hoggart, House of Ill Fame

JAMES CALLAGHAN

As Moses, he would have mistimed his arrival at the parting of the waters.

Austin Mitchell

. . . crude and limited, a rather pedestrian and unprincipled mind. Television news-film alone demonstrated how he deals with foreign statesmen: he bows and grins frequently and is constantly touching his guests, rather like an over-solicitous butler guiding them on their way.

Patrick Cosgrave

MICHAEL FOOT

A kind of walking obituary for the Labour Party.

Peter Jenkins

Looks like a squawking cockatoo, his spiky white strands quivering with indignation as if somebody had just pinched a cuttlefish from his cage.

James Murray, Daily Express

To an American it was incredible . . . that this man who looked like an eccentric professor of ornithology could run for Prime Minister!

Norman Mailer, Mail on Sunday

SIR IAN GILMOUR

A philosopher Tory—like 'military intelligence', a contradiction in terms.

Michael Foot

EDWARD HEATH

Margaret Thatcher and Ted Heath both have a great vision. The difference is that Margaret Thatcher has a vision that Britain will one day be great again, and Ted Heath has a vision that one day Ted Heath will be great again.

*Robert Jones, later MP for Hertfordshire West,
at 1981 Conservative Conference*

Receiving support from Ted Heath in a by-election is like being measured by an undertaker.

George Gardiner

If Ted saw Maggie walking on water he'd say it proves she can't swim.

Westminster joke

MICHAEL HESELTINE

No one can be against him and be all bad.

Edward Pearce

PATRICK JENKIN

A barrister by training and a bungler by experience.

Hugo Young, The Guardian

SIR KEITH JOSEPH

The lamest of lame ducks.

Giles Radice

In a Cabinet of incompetents, he is clearly the most incompetent (except for Michael Heseltine).

Gerald Kaufman

NORMAN ST JOHN STEVAS

The outstanding surviving example of English baroque.

Michael White, quoted by Andrew Roth

NORMAN COULDN'T DECIDE BETWEEN THE CHURCH AND THE MUSIC HALL SO HE BECAME AN MP

Dog Eats Dog

JEFFREY ARCHER

Proof of the proposition that in each of us lurks one bad novel.

Julian Critchley, Westminster Blues

TONY BENN

A johnny-come-lately in left-wing views.

Norman Buchan, quoted by The Sun

JOHN BIFFEN

Mr Tebbit is a fully integrated member of the Cabinet . . . Mr Biffen is . . . semi-detached.

Downing Street press spokesman after Mr Biffen's TV 'balanced ticket' plea

JAMES CALLAGHAN

Skilful in debate, persuasive in speech, and disastrous at his job.

Woodrow Wyatt, Turn Again, Westminster

EDWINA CURRIE

Reminds me of the expression my mother used: 'empty vessels make the most noise.'

Anne Winterton after Mrs Currie's 'some women MPs sit back and look decorative' jibe

EDWARD HEATH

He envies me two things. First, I am a *gentleman*. Second, I have a *first-class* degree.

Lord Hailsham, quoted by Andrew Roth, Heath and the Heathmen

MICHAEL HESELTINE

Tends not to be able to see a parapet without ducking below it. . . . Doing his famous impression of Clint Eastwood playing Mussolini.

Julian Critchley

ROBERT KILROY-SILK

He seems to have lost his marbles.

Martin Flannery after the former Mr Bob Silk's appointment as a TV host

NEIL KINNOCK

Is politically intelligent, has character and courage . . . but has never been made a Minister, lacks experience, and people know it.

Denis Healey, embarrassing aside to
La Stampa *of Italy*

DENNIS SKINNER

Turns being objectionable into a showbiz gimmick.

Austin Mitchell, Westminster Man

In the Wings

GLENYS KINNOCK

The Labour Party is being led by a woman and she is leading them by the nose.

Edwina Currie

KEN LIVINGSTONE

I thought he looked so ugly. I used to put blankets over his head and tell people not to disturb him.

Mrs Ethel Livingstone quoted by
John Carvel, Citizen Ken

IAN PAISLEY

A democrat at Westminster and a demagogue in Belfast.

Merlyn Rees

PETER ROBINSON

Cold, clinical and utterly destructive.

Seamus Mallon

ARTHUR SCARGILL

That man couldn't negotiate his way out of a toilet.

Ray Lynk, Notts UDM Leader

Asking him to have nothing to do with the Militant tendency is like asking Terry Wogan not to appear on television.

John Cartwright, SDP Chief Whip

BERNARD WEATHERILL (MR SPEAKER)

Never cared much for the fellow. Made me a terrible suit once.

Roy Jenkins (Mr Weatherill was, of course, a tailor by trade)

DEIDRE WOOD (LABOUR CANDIDATE AT GREENWICH)

A dumpy figure with large glasses, she looks very much like a plodder. But she does have an advantage over George Howarth, the controversial Labour victor in the Knowsley by-election. He appeared to have no chin; she has two.

Tony Dawe, Daily Express

Double Acts

Arsenic and Old Lace	Mrs Thatcher and President Reagan
Rambo and Rambina	Mrs Thatcher and Norman Tebbit (*by Chris Buckland*)
Haddock	Roy Hattersley and Neil Kinnock (geddit!!) (*by Ken Livingstone*)
The Steptoe and Son of British politics	Michael Foot and Roy Hattersley (*by David Steel*)
Bossyboots *v* the drinker's friend	*Alan Watkins on the Owen/Jenkins SDP leadership contest*
The one with the fat lips *v* the one with no lips	Jimmy Carter *v* Ronald Reagan (*by Raquel Welch*)
Hinge and Bracket	David Owen and David Steel (*by Roy Hattersley*)
Dr David Fudge and Mr David Mudge	(*by Denis Healey*)

Like Hinge and Bracket without the music	Mrs Thatcher's weekly audience with the Queen (*anon, quoted by Paul Potts*)
Little and Large	David Alton and Cyril Smith
There's poor old Fowler who looks as if he's suffering from famine, and there's Lawson who looks as though he caused it	*Neil Kinnock on the Tories 'Little and Large'. (In the Lords in July 1986, Baroness Trumpington confessed that herself and Baroness Hooper were known by this title after successfully piloting the Social Security Bill through the Upper Chamber)*
The quack and the dead	David Owen and David Steel (*by impressionist Rory Bremner*)

7
Privileged to Abuse

I was only seeking clarification as to whether he was a nut-case.
Anthony Beaumont-Dark when admonished by
the Speaker for an attack on Mr Edward Heath

As politics' supreme theatre, the House of Commons has its moments of tragedy and comedy. And its own rarefied code of abuse. Like the moment in May 1986, when Labour spokesman Peter Snape accused Transport Secretary Mr Nicholas Ridley of being 'a hypocrite' and 'an old Etonian twerp'. Quite unparliamentary. He was immediately asked by the Speaker to withdraw the word 'hypocrite'.

There are still echoes of the great parliamentary exchanges of the past, however. Newly-appointed parliamentary private secretary Mr Tim Smith (C, Beaconsfield)—then a rare speaker—was greeted on his elevation in 1984 by Shadow Home Secretary Gerald Kaufman with the words:

I knew the Honourable Gentleman had learned to crawl. But I did not know he had learned to speak.

Mr Brian Sedgemore (Lab, Hackney and Shoreditch) did not quite match up to this mastery of the language when in December 1985 he called Chancellor Mr Nigel Lawson 'a snivelling little git'. (Later, on television, he said he was wrong to use that form of words. He should have said 'snivelling *big* git'.)

Mr Lawson gave as good as he got: 'To call you a pest would be unfair on pests,' he told Mr Sedgemore.

Less reported are the more dignified and subtle exchanges of parliamentary wit in which British politicians still excel:

MR MARK HUGHES: Does the Hon Gentleman accept that many people in the diocese of Durham welcome their Bishop's forthright views on the pressures involved on families consequent on the present strike?

SIR WILLIAM VAN STRAUBENZEE (answering for the Church Commissioners): I hope that the Hon Gentleman recognizes that, not only today but previously, I have attempted to understand both sides. Perhaps he and I—he is much more qualified than I am in this matter—understand the difference between a quip or a phrase used round an academic table and instruction or guidance given by the bishop of a diocese.

MR NORMAN ST JOHN STEVAS: As my Hon Friend is the nearest thing, with the possible exception of myself, to an English pope, would he tell us how many redundant bishops there are in the diocese of Durham?

SIR WILLIAM VAN STRAUBENZEE: None, yet, Sir.

Hansard, November 1984

In June 1986, in the Scottish Grand Committee, one Labour MP suggested that, after the next election, there would only be one Tory MP left in the whole of Scotland, the much-attacked Bill Walker (Tayside North).

Mr Dewar replied drily that he didn't accept there would be even one Tory MP after the election. The suggestion that Mr Walker would still be there 'ignored the personal factor' he opined.

While in Opposition former Transport Minister John Peyton (now Lord Peyton of Yeovil) took part in some famous exchanges with Harold Wilson. Pressing the Prime Minister after a visit to France to see President De Gaulle he observed:

His answers amount to a sort of soliloquy by a rather run-down Hamlet

which led Mr Wilson to call him 'the second gravedigger opposite'.

Later, Mr Wilson visited Washington and took part in a much-publicized 'musical evening' at the White House. Asking him if he had explained to President Johnson just how Britain was wriggling out of its foreign obligations, Mr Peyton observed:

He must have been very relieved that the repertoire of songs offered to him did not include 'Run, Rabbit, Run'.

Another master of the well-crafted parliamentary insult is the Labour left-winger, Mr Eric Heffer. After Mr Robin Maxwell-Hyslop had been rubbing in at great length his point that the Aircraft and Shipbuilding (Nationalisation) Bill was 'hybrid' and therefore fell foul of the parliamentary timetable, Mr Heffer responded:

Mr Speaker, is it in order for the Hon Gentleman to be so pleased that, after raising hundreds of points of order in the time we have been in the House together, he has been right *just once*? [Labour cheers.]

One who came unstuck was Mr Frank Haynes (Lab, Ashfield) who, in February 1982, suddenly shouted at Mr Bill Rodgers the word 'twister'.

'Is it in order for my Hon Friend to call the Hon Gentleman a twister?' inquired Mr Arthur Lewis (Lab, West Ham).

'You cannot be a twister and an Hon Gentleman,' ruled the Speaker.

'Oh yes, you can,' said the worldly-wise Mr Ian Mikardo. 'It's an honourable and noble profession in the textile industry.'

Another favourite of mine is the row over Mr Norman Tebbit's alleged branding of Michael Foot as 'a rat', in June 1976. (He had, in fact, intended this remark to describe Mr Foot's predecessor, Aneurin Bevan.) Mr Tebbit clambered from the mire with this:

If it makes it easier for the House, Mr Deputy Speaker, I will say that the expression I used was 'not that rat'. I specified no particular person. If it will make it easier I will use the words 'one of those who are lower than vermin', to employ a phrase used by the former member for Ebbw Vale.

If such an exchange nowadays seems improbable, consider these classics from the Commons' illustrious past.

First, the case of Dame Florence Horsbrugh's sausages. Miss Horsbrugh had been going on at some length as to how strongly she felt that the British housewife should have a choice in sausages. The boredom was too much for Hugh Dalton who boomed:

What do we do with a sausage! The same thing they do with bananas at Girton!

Miss Horsbrugh was a model of decorum. Pretending only to hear the word 'bananas' she replied:

I hear someone shout 'bananas' and I should like to talk about the nutritional value of bananas, but that would be out of order.

Indeed.

There is also the revered story about the ex-MP and diehard Arabist, Mr Christopher Mayhew. He was giving a forceful speech on international relations when he suddenly blurted out: 'I will give £5,000 to anybody who can prove the Arabs have ever said they would drive the Jews into the sea.'

There was only a moment's silence before a wag on the floor of the House chimed: 'If I hear six—then we can do business.'

8

Six Great Insult-hurlers of Today

Norman Tebbit—the Man with the Fixed-bayonet Smile

Tory tough-nut Norman 'Slugger' Tebbit staged one of the most spectacular rises of the Thatcher years, from being a humble Under-Secretary at the Trade Department to becoming unofficial deputy Prime Minister, and much of it was due to his mastery of invective. His London accent, hard-line approach and ruthless parliamentary wit marked him out as the first of a new league of Conservative leaders: the no-nonsense chairman and MP ready to go down to the shop floor and give as good as he got.

It is a mistake to think of 'the Chingford skinhead' as a leather-jacketed hooligan. Mr Tebbit's repertoire is an astonishing one, with verbal bayonet charge and calculated sneer only two weapons in an arsenal which includes long, dry, logical *reductio ad absurdum*, comparisons with English Test team performances (a favourite), and even parables dressed up as tales of Sherlock Holmes.

His abrasiveness first became a legend when, in November 1977, convalescent Labour MP Tom Litterick said he had been told 'why don't you go and have another heart attack?' (Mr Tebbit's version is that he warned Mr Litterick not to get excited, *in case* he had a heart attack.) As the man who reshaped Britain's employment laws, his most relished target was the trade unions, whose excesses demonstrably set his blood a-boiling: 'I use the word "neuter" when talking about what I'm doing to the unions because I've been told I must not use the vernacular.'

The acidity of his wit is the Tebbit trademark. When Labour spokesman Stanley Orme accused him of stabbing British Leyland in the back, he shot back: 'It's the first time anyone has been stabbed in the back with a cheque book.' He told Denis Healey during the 1983 election campaign that he had become 'hysterical' and should 'take a sedative'. Appearing in 1983 at then beleaguered TV-AM, Mr Tebbit made an exaggerated show

44

of checking all his pockets and saying: 'Just making sure you haven't got my wallet.'

The Brighton bomb denied his health but soon he was back to the form that made him star of the party conferences, telling Dennis Skinner: 'As usual, you have spent more time with your mouth open rather than your ears.' And squashing Neil Kinnock ('I could eat you for breakfast'): 'I'm older than you are, sonny, and you can take me on when you grow up.'

Unveiling his likeness at Madame Tussauds, Mr Tebbit was asked: 'Do you think the Opposition will be able to cope with two of you?' Pointing to the wax dummy he exclaimed: 'This one could cope with most of the Opposition on its own.'

Some favourite Tebbitry:

On Neil Kinnock:

More gimmicks than guts. I wonder whether he exists at all, or if he is some plastic puppet squeezed into shape by his PR experts and by trade union leaders, or whoever bullied him last.

On the unemployed:

Those who stand outside the town hall and scream and throw rotten eggs are not the real unemployed. If they were really hard up, they would be eating them.

On Roy Hattersley:

Would you want him as your bank manager?

On the Labour leadership:

Conceived by those with jelly backbones for those with jelly backbones and brains to match.

On the Alliance's 'going for Gold':

Third best. It is called going for bronze I believe.

To David Owen:

You know I'm a good fisherman. Like all good anglers, I play for big fish and ignore the tiddlers.

Neil Kinnock—the Welsh Wisecracker

Labour Leader Neil Kinnock is not normally bracketed among the most silken-tongued parliamentary wits but his slate-hewn Celtic humour makes him a 'natural' storyteller. He is aggressive to his enemies, but ever ready with a wisecrack, calling Prince Philip, for example, 'a retired naval officer with no visible means of support' (variation, Sir Keith Joseph has 'a mind without any visible means of support'), while former Education Minister Mark Carlisle was dismissed as 'a wet now drying out . . . a mouse now learning to be a rat'.

The humour owes much to the club comic: 'I never knew what the Tories meant when they said inflation was bottomless until Chancellor Geoffrey Howe lost his trousers on the train.' On other occasions it displays the Labour Leader's male machismo, for example, on Peter Tatchell: 'I'm not in favour of witch hunts but I do not mistake bloody witches for fairies.'

Perhaps the most celebrated invective came against David Owen whom the 'Welsh wizard' said possessed 'an ego fat on arrogance and drunk on ambition'.

Elsewhere it is knockabout stuff, like the time he said to the policeman who attended his M4 crash: 'Enough of this "sir" nonsense. My name's Neil. What's yours?' 'Oliver,' replied the officer. 'Well, that's another fine mess you've got me into,' ragged Mr Kinnock.

A favourite with the man whose tales would be lapped up in any bar-room is the set-piece joke. The 'Bedwellty boyo' came to power partly on the strength of two of these: First, Denis Thatcher's alleged passing away. 'Did he utter any last words?' 'No,' came the reply, 'she was with him to the end.'

The second tale was of how Roy Jenkins approached a group of mining MPs during the Labour leadership contest and asked one if he could count on his vote. 'Nay lad,' was the reported reply. 'We're all Labour here.'

Some other favourite Kinnockisms:

On Sir Geoffrey Howe:

Mrs Thatcher's glove puppet.

On Michael Meacher (according to Jilly Cooper):

Kind, scholarly, innocuous—and as weak as hell.

On Dr David Owen:

Purveying retread Thatcherism.

On David Owen again:

What we need in politics is common sense. And the man's arrogant, orthopaedically arrogant in every corpuscle.

On Harold Wilson:

A petty bourgeois, and will remain so in spirit even if made a viscount.

On the ill-fated Conservative Centre Forward group:

Probably the only platoon in history to end the week, without combat, smaller than when it started out.

Finally, during his December, 1986 visit to Washington Mr Kinnock was challenged by an American TV reporter when he called Mrs Thatcher 'a dummy'. 'She is very popular here,' said his inquisitor.

'In that case,' said the Labour leader, 'you can have her then.'

John Biffen—'Biffo' the Bear-tamer

It is he who is credited by colleagues as having come up with the greatest put-down of the Thatcher years. Leader of the House John Biffen (Dr Morgan's, Bridgwater) silenced professional proletarian Dennis Skinner (Tupton Hall) with the devastating: 'We grammar school boys must keep together.'

It was not the only time the quiet, gnomic Mr Biffen destroyed the Bear of Bolsover with a single shot. Taunted by Mr Skinner over Leon Brittan ('Hey ho, he's striking at goal,') the Somerset-born Shropshire lad hit back with: 'There are worse places to strike at.' He was also heard to mutter of the Ruskin-educated emperor of inverted snobbery: 'He's perfect House of Lords material.'

The soft-spoken booking-office clerk for the 'balanced ticket' was an ineffective Treasury Minister but came to win his place in every parliamentarian's heart as Leader of the Commons with the dryest of humour and an agnostic attitude to Thatcherism ('you can tell he doesn't believe what he's defending by the tone of his voice').

He endears himself to opponents by his readiness to prick pomposity. Asked at Prime Minister's Question Time by Tory MP Tony Marlow to debunk Scarmanism, 'the act of only policing at the level acceptable to the most aggressive member of a neighbourhood', Mr Biffen replied that Mr Scarman was from Shropshire, and 'therefore not for debunking'.

The thoughts of Comrade Biffen:

I didn't go into politics to be a kamikaze pilot.

Bogus points of order are the original sin—if they were abolished, life would be all the sadder.

There's no fallen angel like a born-again Tory.

I do not walk hopefully, I walk blindfold.

On a leaked document:

Secrecy is something we all aspire to.

On Edward Heath's promotion of his friends to his Shadow Cabinet:

He seems to have been devoting more time to the Scriptures— he has come up with the strategy of forming the Shadow Cabinet in his own image.

On his loyalty to Mrs Thatcher:

As for the Hon Gentleman's good-natured words, let me disabuse him. I am a shameless bosses' nark and always have been. I wouldn't do the job on any other basis.

On Roy Hattersley:

I have a tremendous affection for him. He fits classically into a Macmillan definition of a politician—they're either bookies or bishops. The Rt Hon Gentleman is a bookie for most of the days of the week and a bishop on Fridays, Thursdays, Wednesdays, or whenever it suits him. Today was a bishop day.

LABOUR SPOKESMAN, to Biffen (while Treasury Minister): As the

Chancellor of the Exchequer has arranged against his policies the TUC, the CBI, the chairman of ICI, two former Prime Ministers and the Secretary of State for Defence, does he not think he might be wrong?

JOHN BIFFEN: The more the Rt Hon Gentleman elaborated that list, the more confidence I gained in my honourable and learned friend.

Denis Healey—the Big, Bad Wolf

He is the Maestro of the political metaphor, the King of the kickabout, the Ayatollah of insult. In Opposition, the last of Labour's 'big men' has shown a remarkable talent for abuse, notably in his own field of foreign affairs but with a special place as chief antagonist of what he has long called 'punk monetarism' (Nigel Lawson being 'the sado-monetarist Chancellor'). 'Big' Denis is by far the most quotable critic of Mrs Thatcher, on South Africa calling her 'an assiduous acolyte of the Botha charm school'. 'Her flash-in-the-pan summer recovery will be just a piece of summer lightning,' he meanwhile proclaimed on the economy.

The Social Democrats too have felt the lash of Mr Healey's bubolic tongue, Roy Jenkins being characterized as 'the David Frost of British politics'. Told that the Social Democrats were attempting to solve problems 'by being nice to them', Healey remarked: 'Not while David Owen's around.'

Denis's impressive repertoire has stretched to members of his own party's left wing, claiming once in public, according to Simon Hoggart, that 'Healey without Benn would be like Torvill without Dean'. In private he explained that: 'When I say we are inseparable I mean I can't get the bugger off my back.'

On being told Mr Benn had proclaimed himself Deputy Leader, Mr Healey said: 'Yes, and tomorrow he is parachuting into Scotland to hold peace talks with the Duke of Hamilton.'

The Reagan administration have long been Healey bugbears. Told that hawkish Assistant Secretary of Defence Richard Perle was coming to London for talks, Mr Healey gave a startled colleague this note: 'Give my sincere regards to Richard Perle and tell him that I would like nothing better than to take a large pair of rusty garden shears and cut his balls off.' That is not to say Mr Healey is pro-Soviet. It is he who stepped off a plane at Moscow and greeted his Politburo reception committee with: 'Ah! Same old Mafia, I see.'

On President Reagan:

> Feels he's fighting Star Wars. He's the Return of the Jedi fighting Darth Vader.

On Mrs Thatcher:

> I think, basically, she's hijacked the Tory Party from the landowners and given it to the estate agents.

Typical of the punch-swinging Healey style was a speech on the Libyan bombing in April 1986, which included this gem:

> The Prime Minister told us yesterday—and this is a matter for a connoisseur of *Yes, Minister*—when asked whether they were privy to a decision . . . 'we have acted together in knowledge of one another's views'. We always assume that the Prime Minister knows her colleagues' views and we usually assume that she ignores them.

Nicholas Fairbairn—a Talent to Amuse

Long entertaining his fellows with the demeanour of Edwardian melodrama, Nicholas Fairbairn, QC, MP, and a tongue-massively-in-cheek Cowardesque wit, polished his dapper style as a successful Scottish advocate before being adopted Conservative candidate, in succession to Sir Alec Douglas-Home, for Kinross and West Perthshire. ('In this rather staid area, I feel rather like a hot-cross bun in a deep freeze.')

Mr Fairbairn's admirers have long marvelled at his inventive *Who's Who* entries. His hobbies have variously been 'ornitholatry' (bird fancying, not bird watching); 'the cure and eradication of the British tick fever' (i.e. our frenzy for credit); 'being blunt and sharp at the same time'; and 'making love, ends meet, and people laugh' ('I think most people if they were honest will admit that those were their main recreations—apart perhaps from Ted Heath who would probably miss out the first and the third').

Much given to wearing a sporran, kilt and skean-dhu, he is, of course, a Scottish patriot. Opposing his own Government's Sunday Shopping Bill, the larger-than-life Mr Fairbairn put forward the motion: 'That this House declined to give a Second Reading to a Bill which provides for English privileges which the Scots have enjoyed since time immemorial and which the English do not deserve.'

Pressed by Labour MP Dennis Canavan for his learned opinion, 'Dandy Nick' offered a pact—he would make his learned opinion available 'if the Hon Gentleman would forgo his ignorant ones'. In his famous fluoridation exchanges with Mrs Edwina Currie, she asked: 'Is my Hon and Learned Friend saying that no one ever died under general anaesthetic for dental treatment?' He replied: 'If that is the basis of my Hon Friend's argument, I can only say that I hope she will take a general anaesthetic frequently.'

Accused by auld enemy Mr Canavan of 'rushing and abrasively attacking a peaceful picket line' of MPs protesting about council rent increases, Mr Fairbairn retorted: 'I certainly take the view that you, who know more about madness and rushing than anyone else, should continue your career as merchant of discourtesy elsewhere.' Though my favourite example of Mr Fairbairn's badinage was his description of Mr Frank Dobson, Labour MP for Holborn and St Pancras, as 'the Hon Member for the two tube stations'.

Some further examples of the Fordell wit:

On office:

> *Yes, Minister* is a gross disexaggeration. Ministers are not even puppets on strings today. They are the fifth little herring on the end of the rod.

On Edward Heath:

A little boy sucking his misogynist thumb and blubbing and carping in the corner of the front bench below the gangway is a mascot which Parliament can do without.

To Sam Silkin, Attorney General, on the Community Land Bill:

I do not believe the Minister understands what his amendment means. I certainly don't, and I am a mere Scotsman, a mere lawyer, a mere QC in Scotland, and so I am an idiot.

Dennis Skinner—the Derbyshire Dangermouse

The destructive tactics of the bright scholarship boy who became the Commons' heckler-in-chief, Dennis Skinner, in fact belie an intellectual background and a ready wit. Yet it is for shouting down the Opposition that the 'Beast of Bolsover' (a term, to his chagrin, ruled unparliamentary by Speaker George Thomas) has become known as he taunts Tories and Social Democrats from his lair on the front rank of the Labour benches just below the gangway.

Shouting 'Get stuffed!' 'Commissar, Gauleiter' and 'Heil Hitler' to Michael Heseltine, is the sort of premature ejaculation that has, paradoxically, made this self-styled parliamentary hooligan a favourite with the trendy Filofax generation he loathes so much. Yet his interventions can be subtle. It was he alone who noticed a calculated attempt in 1983 to soften Mrs Thatcher's image, exclaiming: 'She's changed her voice again! Janet Brown Mark II!!!'

Raising a point of order about the 1970s with Speaker George Thomas brought the response: 'I cannot answer. I was busy with Welsh affairs at the time.' 'Yes, and you were making a mess of that, too,' retorted The Beast.

We can always rely on him for humour, like the time he yelled to Roy Hattersley after a conference on Freedom of Information: 'There'll be fresh air in the corridors of Westminster, Roy.' 'I'll be blowing it,' replied a genial Hattersley. 'From the right end, I hope,' said Mr Skinner.

Typical thoughts of Chairman Dennis:

To Paul Channon:

You're educated beyond your intelligence.

To Shirley Williams:

You are living off the immoral earnings of the Labour Party.

On the SDP's 'Council for Social Democracy':

The Council for Social Diseases.

9

The Professionals' Choice: Great Exchanges

Every politician, whether parliamentarian, statesman, organizer or trades unionist, has his or her favourite memory of cut and thrust:

PADDY ASHDOWN, MP
Yeovil (Lib)

In one meeting to discuss the differences on defence between Liberals and the SDP, following Dr David Owen's recent and, for many, unwelcome pronouncements, I recall that somebody said that they thought Dr Owen was a Gaullist. This drew back the comment from another participant to the effect that, no, he was an 'own goalist'!

HENRY BELLINGHAM, MP
Norfolk North West (C)

HB, during my maiden speech: I have no intention of emulating one of my less illustrious kinsmen, one John Bellingham, who holds the distinction of being the only Englishman to have assassinated a Prime Minister.
LABOUR FRONT-BENCH SPOKESMAN (*unreported* in Hansard): I don't know why not—you would be doing all of us a great service!

RON BROWN, MP
Edinburgh Leith (Lab)

Speaker George Thomas, ordering me from the House in 1980 after challenging Nick Fairbairn, then Scottish Solicitor-General: 'I name you . . . who is he? . . . I name you, Ernie Ross!'

Turning to the Speaker, I said: 'I only hope his wife doesn't mind.'

EDWINA CURRIE, MP
Derbyshire South (C)

Dennis Skinner, the Beast of Bolsover, rose on a point of order after Question Time to object to the amount of time given to the Leader of the SDP, Dr David Owen.

'I want to know, Mr Speaker, why this 'ere pompous git gets so much time . . .' he started, but the Speaker was on him in a flash. 'The Honourable Gentleman is an experienced parliamentarian, and he knows he must withdraw those words,' he insisted.

Dennis rose to his feet again, brow furrowed in thought. After a moment he sighed: 'In deference to you then, Mr Speaker, I will withdraw "pompous".'

During the debate on fluoridation in 1985, Mr Nicholas Fairbairn was a fierce opponent, while I, having been involved with the NHS for some years, was a firm supporter.

Nicholas was at pains to prove that fluoride was a poison and therefore should be kept out of water supplies. 'But could I point out to the Honourable Gentleman,' I intervened, 'that almost anything is a poison if taken in sufficient quantity, and that the amount of fluoride to be added is minute? If, for example, we were to spreadeagle the Honourable Gentleman on the floor of this House, and pour sufficient water into him, then it would kill him very quickly.'

He fixed me with a baleful glare. 'I cannot imagine what

would be worse,' he said, 'being spreadeagled by the Honourable Lady or having all that unadulterated pure water poured down my throat.'

GEOFFREY DICKENS, MP
Littleborough and Saddleworth (C)

The following exchange was during a statement to the House on a rape case. Speaker George Thomas allowed only a few questions from each side.

GEOFFREY DICKENS: Point of order, Mr Speaker.

SPEAKER: If you seek to extend questions you will do me a favour, the House a favour and yourself a favour if you remain in your seat.

DICKENS: Mr Speaker, I seek to do a favour for every woman in the United Kingdom.

The House fell about laughing at this for some minutes.

SPEAKER: It was well worth calling the Hon Member. I am bursting to know what his point of order is.

ROBERT ATKINS: So are all the women.

(Uncontrollable laughter.)

NICHOLAS FAIRBAIRN, MP
Perth and Kinross (C)

In 1980, Norman Buchan, Labour MP for Renfrew West, put down an amendment during the committee stage of the Criminal Justice Bill that 'no lawyer or judge or any other shall be in future asked to wear wigs, gowns or uniforms of any kind'. His argument was that such outdated paraphernalia was 'a crutch for the dignity of its lawyers'.

Having argued that the purpose of all uniform and dress is to identify the *office* of the wearer and subject his personality to his duties, I came to the matter and replied: 'Why, for instance does the Hon Member wear a tie? Why, if it comes to it, does he wear trousers? Is it in order to have a crutch for his dignity or to protect the dignity of his crutch.'

GEORGE FOULKES, MP
Carrick, Cumnock and Doon Valley (Lab)

The Prime Minister, droning on at Prime Minister's Questions in her best (worst?) schoolmistress tones, made the mistake of pausing. Shouted an irreverent Labour heckler: 'Come on, this is "Question Time" not *Listen with Mother*.'

JOHN GOLDING
General Secretary, National Communications Union,
former MP for Newcastle under Lyme (Lab)

Once when I was going on and on talking on one Bill, to make sure the next measure was never reached, a Tory member got up and said: 'On a point of order, Mr Speaker, the Hon Gentleman doesn't know what he's talking about.' I told Mr Selwyn Lloyd that this was not a point of order. Nowhere in the rules of the House of Commons was it required that an MP should know what he was talking about. If there was, there would hardly be any discussion! I was allowed to continue.

JOAN MAYNARD, MP
Sheffield Brightside (Lab)

In the Commons Chamber a Tory told Martin Redman to take his hands out of his pockets (Martin was asking a supplementary to the Prime Minister). Quick as a flash, Norman Atkinson said to the Tory: 'The trouble is you have your hands in everybody's pocket.'

LORD MURRAY OF EPPING FOREST
former General Secretary of the TUC

Roy Hattersley was attacking Norman St John Stevas for not having enough courage of his convictions that the Government was wrong on the issue of sanctions. He quoted St John Stevas as saying that there was no point in putting down a motion of no confidence unless there was some prospect of it being passed. 'It is difficult to imagine,' declared Hattersley 'a more frank statement of the triumph of tactics over principle.

St John Stevas rose: 'The Right Hon Gentleman asked the House whether we could think of a better example of the triumph of tactics over principle than my statement. Has the Rt Hon Gentleman,' he asked, 'considered his own career?'

GERRY NEALE, MP
Cornwall North (C)

On concluding a speech to Cornish farmers, I said '. . . so, on average, I do not think you are doing too badly.'

'Look here, mister,' reacted one of the audience, leaping to his feet. 'Stand me with my left foot in a block of ice and my right foot in a bucket of boiling water and tell me on average I am all right and I'll bloody tell you I ain't.'

MATTHEW PARRIS
former Conservative MP, now presenter of LWT's
Weekend World

During the passage of the Sexual Offences ('kerb-crawling') Bill through Committee Stage in 1985, David Mellor (the Junior Home Office Minister) who was progressing the Bill, accused me (who was opposing it) of: 'Putting up arguments only to knock them down; of conducting a debate with himself.' I replied: 'The Hon Gentleman accuses me of conducting an argument with myself. Maybe so; but one has to have some kind of an intellectual challenge in this place!'

JAMES PRIOR
former Leader of the Commons, Secretary of State for
Agriculture, Employment and Northern Ireland

I had this memorable exchange with Labour MP Andrew Faulds on the last Thursday before the General Election of 1974:
MR FAULDS: As his last stint before he loses his job permanently, will the Rt Hon Gentleman make speedy arrangements to have erected on one of the plinths out there in the Members' Lobby a rubber statue of the immediately ex-Prime Minister bearing the words, carved in stone, 'The Wrecker'?
MR PRIOR: I have been longing to have a chance to reply to the Hon Gentleman. I hope that he will have a good chance to go back to the job which he occupied before and take part in another film such as *Young Winston* in which he played the part of a mounted Boer.

SIR MICHAEL SHAW, MP
Scarborough (C)

At the start of the Standing Committee sitting on the 1982 Finance Bill, the Opposition began by seeking to raise a number of points of order, the content of which appeared to me to be both doubtful and likely to be lengthy. I felt it right, therefore, as chairman, to seek to cut them without destroying the existing good humour of the committee.

After I had restrained one Hon Member, Mr George Foulkes rose to a further point of order, but prefaced it as follows:
MR FOULKES: On a point of order, Sir Michael. I had hoped that it would seem to someone appropriate to congratulate you on your honour. However, I do not rise to congratulate you on it because I do not believe in such honours, although if I did, I should think you the sort of man who should be given one.

THE CHAIRMAN: If I believed in allowing points of order to go on indefinitely, the Hon Gentleman is the sort of Hon Gentleman whom I would allow to go on indefinitely.
MR FOULKES: I think that it is 15-love to you, Sir Michael.

IVOR STANBROOK, MP
Orpington (C)

I once entered the Chamber just as William Walker, seated behind Ted Heath, got up to ask a question. Courteously, I ducked down and found myself kneeling before Ted. 'This hasn't happened for a long time,' he said.

DAVID TRIPPIER, MP
Rossendale and Darwen (C)

The Prime Minister was asked by the Rt Hon Merlyn Rees whether she thought the Rt Hon Peter Walker should resign as a result of a speech he had made which appeared to be disloyal. The answer she gave at the dispatch box was: 'No, I think he should realize what a tolerant Prime Minister he has.'

JOHN WATSON, MP
Skipton and Ripon (C)

I was asked to speak one December at the Annual General Meeting of the Pateley Bridge Conservative Association. Just before the meeting started I mentioned to the chairman that December seemed to be an unusual month for such a Branch AGM. They are normally held in October. He explained that the meeting had indeed been attempted for October but that very few people had turned up and that therefore it had been rearranged for December with 'something of an incentive for people to attend'.

I modestly asked whether I was that incentive. 'No, you're not,' he said. 'We've laid on some crisps and a meat pie.'

10

First Lady for Scorn: Margaret Thatcher

Trying to tell the Prime Minister anything is like making an important phone call and getting an answering machine.

David Steel

One of the longest-serving Prime Ministers of history, Margaret Hilda Thatcher has also found herself the subject of the greatest abuse. Compared unfavourably with despots, dragons and dinosaurs, the 'Iron Lady' ('with metal fatigue'—Denis Healey) has provided the richest crop of insults for the serious student of political invective since Arthur Balfour was dubbed Lisping Hawthorn Bird, Niminy-Piminy and Brutal Bloody Balfour.

The cruellest woman since Lady Macbeth.
Psychologist Dr Douglas Baker of Potters Bar,
quoted by the Sunday Mirror

Reminds me of a refugee from *'Allo 'Allo*, scuttling from safe house to safe house as she nervously circles the real problems of life.

Donald Dewar

If you want Margaret Thatcher to change her mind you don't use argument—you look for a transplant surgeon.

John Edmonds

The reasons can be put as:
1 the brusque manner of her election;
2 the sometimes unwelcome fact that she is a woman;
3 snobbery at her lower middle-class origins;
4 plain jealousy from those overlooked for preferment;
5 just as plain jealousy from women;
6 her tough and uncompromising style.

Insulting for the wets in at least some of those categories is Mr Julian Critchley, Tory MP for Aldershot, who declared himself 'not one of us' in dramatic style, anonymously penning a ruthlessly critical article in the *Observer*, confessing his guilt, and then developing a lucrative career as a Thatcher baiter (it cannot have comforted No. 10 that he writes, it must be said, exceedingly well).

According to Mr Critchley, the Grantham Grocer's daughter was 'tart, obstinate, and didactic', and 'continually demanded the price of everything while remaining ignorant of its value'. He said the combination of her 'gritty voice' and her 'fierce and unrelenting glare' plus her repetition of the obvious 'amounted to the infliction of pain'. Most cutting of all was, however, his remark that having lunch or dinner with the Prime Minister 'churned the gastric juices in the most frightful way' and was 'to be avoided at all costs'.

1 Surprise Elevation

One of the more telling comments came from a senior Tory on Mrs Thatcher's enthronement. 'We might as well give the filly a run,' he observed. (The underlying message being that a bullet and the knacker's yard beckoned if the form horse showed any signs of becoming lame.)

It wasn't an election. It was an assumption.
Norman St John Stevas on her
taking over the leadership

2 Male Chauvinism

I think she may need to put up a tough appearance to compensate for the fact she is not a man . . .
Andrew Faulds

She is a woman and, as a woman in power, is constantly trying to prove herself. I hate to say this, but I am sure it is the problem.
Norman St John Stevas

3 Snobbery

In the words of Mr Critchley, as Mrs Thatcher went up in the

world, 'so the party went down'. The Military Cross gave way to Rotary Club badges, he lamented, and the knights of the shires gave way to estate agents and accountants.

If she has a weakness it is for shopkeepers, which probably accounts for the fact that she cannot pass a branch of Marks and Spencer without inviting the manager to join her private office.

Julian Critchley

I wouldn't say she was open-minded on the Middle East, so much as empty-headed. She probably thinks Sinai is the plural of Sinus.

Jonathan Aitken

4 The Disinherited

Beaten incumbent Edward Heath told a Turkish newspaper in 1984: 'Whatever the lady does is wrong. I do not know of a single right decision taken by her.' He must have longed for the old days at Cabinet when he was able to tell her: 'That's quite enough, Margaret.'

Working with a team is not her strong point.

David Howell, axed Cabinet minister

Her first Treasury team had no experience of running a whelk stall, let alone a decent-sized business.

James Prior

5 Female Jealousy?

Dame Janet Vaughan, tutor at Somerville, told radio listeners loftily that her former charge was 'a perfectly good second-class chemist, a Beta chemist . . . she wasn't an interesting person, except as a Conservative . . . I would never, if I had amusing, interesting people staying, have thought of asking Margaret Thatcher.'

Although we were not displeased in the Labour lady members' room when Margaret Thatcher got the Opposition leadership, we knew that she was what the American feminists irreverently call 'a man with tits' and would do little if nothing either for women in the House or for women outside it.

Maureen Colquhoun

Mrs Susan Crosland, the Labour Cabinet Minister's widow, meanwhile turned down three overtures from London publishers to pen *The Margaret Thatcher Story*. 'There's really no nuance of personality there at all,' she said tartly. 'Basically no story.'

6 The Iron Lady

In Madame Tussaud's 1983 poll to find the 'most hated dummy', Mrs Thatcher was beaten into third place by Adolf Hitler and Idi Amin—but visitors put her well ahead of Count Dracula and the Yorkshire Ripper in the hate stakes.

She will fight like an alley-cat to her last hour in the Downing Street bunker.

David Owen

Spitting Image was right. She really does treat her Cabinet as vegetables.

Denis Healey (after the satirical TV programme's joke showing a Cabinet dinner. Waiter: What about the vegetables.' Mrs T: 'Oh, they'll have the same as me.')

Perhaps the most tasteless diatribe against Mrs Thatcher came in a January 1986 pop single by the French singer Renaud Sanchan. Part of this went:

There isn't a woman on earth who could be more of a crook
than her brother
More vain or more of a crook—except of course Meesus
Thatcher.

The climax of the mean little ditty was that if M Sanchan stayed on earth he would become a dog 'and as my fire hydrant—use Meesus Thatcher'.

155 Unkind Names for Mrs T

Mrs Thatcher attracts the worst kind of name-calling, of course, and building on the purely chauvinistic, we can aid the curious with a league table of the main culprits:

Leading the field with 13 nicknames is Denis Healey:

Bargain Basement Boadicea
Calamity Jane
Catherine the Great of
  Finchley
The Dragon Empress
Miss Floggie
The Great She-elephant
The Incredible Revolving
  Maggie

The Parrot on Ronald
  Reagan's Shoulder
La Passionara of Middle-class
  Privilege
Pétain in Petticoats
Rambona
Rhoda the Rhino
Winston Churchill in Drag

RATHER GRATIFYING ACTUALLY... I ONLY HAD ONE NICKNAME AT SCHOOL

10

In second place comes Gerald Kaufman with 7:

The Enemy Abroad
The Fishwife
The Gesticulating Pygmy
The Lady with the Iron Heel

President Reagan's Glove
  Puppet
The Thieving Magpie
The Wicked Witch of the West

Matched by:

NEIL KINNOCK (7)

Dictator
An Egotistical Flea in a Fit
St Maggie
High Taxer Thatcher

Senator Thatcher (after US
  Libyan bombing)
The Thatchertollah
Twister

Next comes:

NORMAN ST JOHN STEVAS (5)

The Blessed
The Blessed Margaret
The Blessed One

The Immaculate
  Misconception
The Leaderene

Runners-up in the contest:

EDWARD PEARCE (4)

Baroness Belgrano
Big Mammy Wham-Bang-Big-
  Mammy

Countess of Kesteven
The Finchley Footpad

DENNIS CANAVAN (3)

Dangerous Doll
TBW (That Bloody Woman)

That Demented Woman

THE SUN (3)

Diamond Lil
The Iron Welder

Waggie Thatcher (after beach
  exploits with a puppy)

65

DAVID OWEN (3)

Big Sister   Queen Bee
The Duchess of Dulwich

JULIAN CRITCHLEY (2)

Lady San Carlos   Penelope Keith

ROY HATTERSLEY (2)

Hard-hearted Harridan   Lady Macbeth

PRIVATE EYE (2)

The Boss   The Grocer's Daughter

ARTHUR SCARGILL (2)

Attila the Hen from Number   The Plutonium Blonde
   10

DENNIS SKINNER (2)

Madame Suharto   The Westminster Ripper

Other nicknames scoring one each:

Arthur Daley   *Norman Willis*
Ayesha   *Patrick Jenkin*
The Beached Shark   *Alan Watkins*
Boadicea   *James Prior*
La Bombolla (the doll)   *President Craxi of Italy*
The Bossette   *Lord Carrington*
Calamity Maggie   Daily Mirror
The Cold War Warrior   *Roy Mason*
The Cuckoo of British Politics   *David Steel*
David Owen in Drag   Rhodesia Herald
Dolly Parton   *Julian Barnes*
Mrs Finchley   *From a slip of the tongue by*
                                       David Dimbleby

Glenda Jackson   *Paul Callan*
The Goddess of War and Want   *John Pilger*
Miss Iceberg   Daily Star
The Iceberg   *Cyril Smith*
The Iron Lady   Red Star (*Moscow*)

The Iron Maiden	*First used by Marjorie Proops*
Jezebel	*Rev Ian Paisley*
Madam Maggie 'the biggest Madam of all'	*English Collective of Prostitutes*
Maggots Scratcher	*Steven Berkoff*
Marie Antoinette	*Peter Shore*
The Most Hated Prime Minister	*Tony Benn*
Mother	*Tory back-benchers*
Murderess	*Col Gaddafi*
Nanny of the Nation	*Germaine Greer*
Mrs Nixon	*Labour MPs*
Nurse Maggie	*Jon Akass*
The Old Boot	*From teenager who threw rotten egg*
Old Iron Knickers	*Ron Brown (Leith)*
Old Mrs T	*Joe Ashton*
Our Militant Tendency	*Anon Tory MP (the initials [MT] are the same)*
Mrs Pacman	*Lady Falkender*
Pariah of the World	*Dave Nellist*
The Parrot	*Edward Heath*
A Political Prostitute	*Peter Robinson*
The Poujadiste	*Michael Heseltine, quoted by* The Guardian
Queen Canute	Daily Mirror
Queen of the Litter Louts	*John Edmonds*
Queen Maggie	*Adam Raphael*
The Queen of Sheba	*Lord Stockton*
Queen Tina	*John Torode*
Rambina	*Chris Buckland*
Stupid Woman	*Eric Heffer*
A Surrogate Man	*Glenys Kinnock*
Thane of Cawdor	*Ian Aitken*
The Upas Tree ('the branches may be splendid, but contact may be deadly')	*Roy Jenkins*
The Uranium Lady	*French newspaper*

The largest 'score', however, goes to 'Anon' with:

Aunt Sally (*from* Worzel Gummidge)	The Black Prince
Bambi with Missiles	Mrs Blue Rinse
The Bitch	Miss Bossy
	Bossy Boots

Chief Recruiting Officer for the National Front
The Cold War Bitch
Evita
Frances of Assisi
Gloriana
The Great Executioner
Hard-hearted Hannah
The Headmistress
Heather
Hilda
Imelda
The Iron Butterfly
Joan of Arc
Lady Falklander
The Mad Thatch
Mama Doc
Mrs Marcos
Mark Thatcher's Minder
Much Hairdo about Nothing
My Yiddisher Momma (*after visit to Israel*)
Naggie Thatcher
Old Iron Woman (*left-wing school text-book*)
One-woman Task Force
The Original Cabbage Patch Doll
The Patron Saint of Milliners
Patron Saint of the Rich
Phantom of the Westminster Opera
The Queen of Monetarism
The Reluctant Debutante
Salome of the Suburbs
She Who Must Be Obeyed
Snobby Roberts (*school nickname*)
Stonewall Thatcher
Thatcher Milk-snatcher
Thatch the Hatchet (*wall graffiti*)
That Tiresome Woman
That Woman
Tina—There Is No Alternative
The Tsarina
Wicked Witch of the Western World
The Witch of Finchley
The Wolverine

11

The Politician's Secret Weapon— a Sense of Humour

JOURNALIST KEN SCHAPEL: There's a rumour in Canberra.
SIR ROBERT MENZIES: I'm sure there is.

from The Wit of Sir Robert Menzies

Candidates must be rhinoceros-skinned enough to take a joke. If they have any sense, they will learn how to tell one, too. Westminster has long been its own Palace of Varieties, as can be seen by the inscription above the hot-air hand-drier in a Commons gentleman's cloakroom: 'Press button for message from your MP.'

Roy Hattersley, one of many parliamentarians who can turn a fine humorous phrase, was asked during a debate on football hooliganism: 'Would it not be the solution if they were all made to sit down?'

Quick as a kick and rush-through ball at his beloved Sheffield

Wednesday, he shot back: 'That particular arrangement has never had that effect on the Parliamentary Labour Party.'

Much political humour comes in the form of asides, of course, and here the wit can be without mercy. After a Sunday newspaper carried allegations of spanking sessions at the home of Tory MP Harvey Proctor, Dennis Skinner was moved to ask the House where Proctor was. 'In the Whips' Office,' suggested back-bench colleague Robert Atkins.

Ronald Reagan is one highly successful politician who spins a merry yarn in private company, sometimes to the embarrassment of his guests. One of his favourites is to tell of Leonid Brezhnev on his deathbed whispering to the man who eventually took his post: 'Comrade Andropov—just one last piece of advice. Make sure the Soviet people follow you.'

According to the President, KGB chief Andropov looked at the dying man squarely in the eye and replied: 'Don't worry. If any of them don't follow me—they'll follow you.'

That is only one of a whole line of Russian anecdotes from the right-wing former Governor of California. Another:

The Kremlin is like a baby—it has an appetite at one end and no sense of responsibility at the other.

Other Reagan jibes include:

In Government we need people with a ruthless streak and a capacity to drive a hard bargain—like Brook Shields' mother, Terri.

On David Stockman's proposed economic cuts in 1981:

We won't leave you alone out there, Dave, we'll all come to the hanging.

Another 'Mr Mean' Stockman gag came from Chief of the White House staff, James Baker:

We saved a lot of air conditioning in the White House this summer. We kept cool by huddling round David Stockman's heart.

My own favourite American political jest was of old-time city boss, Richard Croker of New York, though it could be applied to anyone who sits on the fence too long. A man of even less than a few words, Croker joined a boisterous Fourth of July party at

Tammamy Hall but when it came time to sing 'The Star Spangled Banner', stood there stony faced.

'Why isn't he singing?' asked one of the revellers.

Growled an aide: 'He just doesn't want to commit himself.'

Other Americans in the Reagan years have shown an imaginative humorous streak. White House Chief of Staff, Donald Regan, while still Secretary of the Treasury, was accused of saying of Paul Volcker, head of the US Federal Reserve Bank: 'He is obstinate, tyrannical, and a smoker of cheap cigars.'

When the publicity rebounded, Regan apologized. 'I never said anything about his cheap cigars,' he said.

The most unlikely politicians have proved that they too possess the important ingredient of a sense of humour. The owlish Transport Minister, Mr Peter Bottomley, wrote to *The Times* in June 1986 saying:

> You describe me (Diary, June 13) as stalling on the M42. What else do you expect from a politician?

Meanwhile, the Reverend Ian Paisley was all too quick to comment on Mrs Thatcher's finger operation:

> It is the will of God. He has struck down the very hand that signed the Anglo-Irish agreement.

Even Chamber-hooligan-in-chief Dennis Skinner has been known to share a joke. Spying a cavalcade of gleaming Lincoln limousines at the Commons entrance, he inquired of a colleague: 'Who's visiting?'

The guest was American deputy Commander-in-Chief, Mr George Bush, and Mr Skinner was told: 'It's the Vice-President.'

'Oh,' said Mr Skinner. 'I didn't know Mick McGahey was in town.'

Another unexpected comedian is the dour-for-the-cameras TUC General Secretary, Mr Norman Willis. Taking office during one of the sporadic TUC crises, he quipped:

> I've no sleep problems—I sleep like a baby, one hour sleeping and one hour crying.

Managing the TUC, he said, was like 'being a one-legged competitor in a backside-kicking contest'. And while still in competitive spirit, he joked of his colleagues:

> If the TUC entered a javelin-throwing contest, they would elect to receive.

71

In the professional put-down a rich vein of humour can some-times be observed. One exponent of the art, Pierre Trudeau, repulsed criticism of a new swimming pool at the Canadian Prime Minister's official residence in Ottawa with the invitation:

You may come over at any time to practise your diving—preferably before the water is in.

Edward Heath expertly snubbed a grinning, moustachioed figure, who had thanked him for support against the Govern-ment's move to abolish the GLC, with the words: 'Yes, but who are you?' (He must surely have recognized the TV face of the year, Ken Livingstone.)

MP Mr Neville Sanderson, on the way to defecting from Labour to the SDP, put the boot in when his constituency secretary wrote inviting him to join the picket-line of the Left at Grunwick. 'Dear Sir or Madam,' he wrote. 'I am sure the police can manage without my assistance.'

And Denis Healey enjoyed a jape when taking a stroll during one particularly tedious world summit. Approached by a journalist from *The Economist* for a quote, he answered in profuse Italian. The reporter must have thought he was suffering from overwork and, according to Joe Haines in the *Daily Mirror*, told colleagues: 'I had an awful experience. I spoke to someone who thought he was the Chancellor and turned out to be a bloody Italian.'

Three last cruel examples of wit from professionals at the game—fully-fledged comedians—should inspire politician amateurs.

Jasper Carrot on Norman Tebbit:

There's a way of cutting unemployment at a stroke—if only Norman Tebbit would have one.

Who Dares Wins on Ian Paisley:

He's supporting his favourite charity—Orange Aid.

And Bob Monkhouse on Denis Healey:

I saw a headline which read 'Healey caught with his pants down'. I thought, that's a shame—it will make it easier to hear what he's saying.

12

Five Favourite Targets for Venom

He can't decide whether he was born in a log cabin or a manger.
Senator Barry Goldwater on President Reagan

If there ever was a WSPCP (World Society for the Prevention of Cruelty to Politicians) five current figures would surely qualify for lifetime membership: Ronald Reagan, Neil Kinnock, Sir Geoffrey Howe, David Owen and Mrs Edwina Currie. For various reasons in the past five years they have been on the receiving end of a positive transfusion of venom. They may try not to let it show but, without doubt, it stings.

Where's the Rest of Him?

The oldest President to take office, Ronald Reagan may be the man to whom no mud will stick but that is not for the want of his opponents trying. They just throw more. One Congressman showed the lay-it-on-thick approach: 'Ronnie is a loose cannon on the pitching deck of a sinking boat in the midst of a storm at sea.' (Pause to take air.)

The unkind cut was matched by his 1984 opponent, Walter Mondale, who cruelly observed: 'I don't like to attack Reagan as being too old but, remember, in his first movie Gabby Hayes got the girl.'

Presidential brother Neil 'Moon' Reagan was phoned by the Commander-in-Chief after his 1984 TV debate with Walter Mondale. The President asked how brother had thought the contest went. 'If I were you,' said 'Moon', 'I should fire your make-up woman.'

Then there was the unkind joke of the world leaders flying to a summit. In a mid-air crisis, the pilot dramatically announced: 'I'm sorry, but there are only four parachutes for you five passengers.

You must decide democratically who gets to bale out.'

Mrs Thatcher, being a woman, was voted the first 'chute. President Reagan, being the most important person on the plane, naturally was awarded the second. President Andropov, claiming he was just as important, seized upon the third. The Pope murmured that he would put his trust in God, and handed his parachute to the fifth passenger, a hippy stowaway.

'But there is one for each of us,' the hippy replied. 'Reagan took my rucksack.'

Other X-certificate cuts at the 'B-movie actor President'.

It's not true that Ronald Reagan dyes his hair—he's just prematurely orange.

Gerald Ford

Still a bad actor.

Nicholas Von Hoffman, The Spectator

IS IT TRUE SENATOR THAT RONNIE AND NANCY WERE THE MODELS FOR THE 'LOVE-IS' CARTOONS?

So far he's proved Lincoln right. You can't fool all the people some of the time.

Haynes Johnson, Washington Post

Ronald Reagan must love poor people, because he's creating so many more of them.

Edward Kennedy

Has changed from being a B-movie actor into a B-movie President. He will go down in history as one of the few American Presidents who didn't go down in history.

Daily Mirror

If he didn't understand the big picture, how could he make the right decisions?

David Stockman

Ronnie for Governor? Wrong casting! Jimmy Stewart for Governor, Ronnie for best friend.

Jack Warner

A triumph of the embalmer's art.

Gore Vidal

For he's a Jolly Good Bellow

'Neil Kinnock's a strange fellow,' Lord Chapple wrote in the *Daily Mail*. 'Some folk think he's the best orator since Nye Bevan, while others dismiss him as the world's biggest waffler. But to my mind, he speaks like a crab—dealing with problems sideways rather than head on.'

Elected to the Labour Party leadership in a surprise rediscovery of youth and without any ministerial experience, Neil Kinnock is, according to your persuasion, the new John F. Kennedy, 'Saint' Kinnock—or the waffling Welsh windbag, incapable of papering over the vast crevasses in his party created by such issues as Militant.

No one can doubt, however, the success of the early years of his leadership in restoring the shattered morale of his party to bring it to within an ace of winning an election for the first time in twelve years.

One major question mark seemed to be about his ability to emerge on top of world affairs after a series of disastrous overseas visits, including the famed occasion when he accused US Secretary George Shultz of being 'off his pram'. (Presumably he meant 'off his trolley'.) Wrote Ferdinand Mount in the *Daily Telegraph*: 'As soon as he takes off from Heathrow, Mr Kinnock seems to lose all sense of restraint or even self-preservation . . . he misses the point of the exercise, tending to behave like a sailor on shore leave, spraying promises, wisecracks and insults around with hectic abandon.'

What he needs is not an autocue but an autostop.

Anon Labour MP

Reminds me of one of those beauty queen competitors who always smile and say that they want to work with children and travel a lot.

Lord Chapple, Daily Mail

During his visit to Washington in December, 1986, Mr Kinnock came in for an extraordinary tirade of abuse about Labour's 'US bases out' defence policy. A cartoon by Cookson in *The Sun* showed him arriving back at Heathrow firing limply from a peashooter over the caption: 'Looks like he's come up with some more defence ideas.'

At last a British comedian has become a success in America . . . the 'butcher of Broadway' said: 'I take back all I have said about British comedy' . . . the name of this new comic star . . . Neil Kinnock.

Joke on Nicky Campbell show,
Capital Radio (adapted)

Ian Rush has had talks with Juventus this week and says he intends to destroy Europe's defences . . . Neil Kinnock has been in Washington and says he plans to do the same thing.

Joke on Nicky Campbell show,
Capital Radio (adapted)

Neil Kinnock in his new grey suit with the oh-so-tasteful red rose in the buttonhole, walking backwards into socialism as the penniless man walked backwards into the cinema—in the hope that the attendant would think he was leaving it.

Nigel Lawson

Mr Kinnock is certainly a man of promise or rather, to be absolutely honest, a man of promises . . . He is clearly destined for a long career as a promising Leader of the Opposition.

Nigel Lawson again

Or to go really 'bananas' . . .

Whatever has happened to the scrambled mess of cold porridge, loose wires, faulty contacts and old knitting which

76

Neil Kinnock calls his brain? It is already widely recognized that this atrophied organ— nature's answer to a Spanish telephone exchange—is only intermittently connected with his mouth.

'Mills, the Angry Voice', Daily Star

The Thinking Man's Sedative

Ever since Denis Healey got the laughs for saying an attack by him was like being 'savaged by a dead sheep' the woollen label has stuck on mild-mannered Welsh lawyer Sir Geoffrey Howe— as have adjectives like sleepy, dreary, languid, somnambulant, soporific, and nicknames like 'the Iron Sheep', 'Tortoiseshell', and 'Mogadon Man' after the well-loved sleeping pill.

Harangued in front of the TV cameras by Zambian President Kenneth Kaunda, told by the man he recommended for a KBE, anti-hunger campaigner Mr Bob Geldof, that his speech to the UN on aid was 'a load of crap', ticked off by Mrs Thatcher in Cabinet for his attitude on South African sanctions ('If that's the mood you're in, you had better stay at home.'), Sir Geoffrey might, you may think, be tempted one day to do just that.

Even in his most embarrassing moment, misplacing his trousers on an overnight train, brought only ribaldry from his colleagues, one of whom told him the loss had 'revealed your human face'.

CONSTITUENT AT A MEETING: Sir Geoffrey? Aye, he's well kent . . . he's a well-known nonentity.

Ron Brown, MP (Leith)

Q. Why does Sir Geoffrey Howe only need four hours' sleep a night?
A. Because he sleeps standing up.

Conservative back-benchers' joke

How can one best summon up the exquisite, earnest tedium of the speech of Sir Geoffrey Howe in yesterday's South African debate? It was rather like watching a much-loved family tortoise creeping over the lawn in search of a distant tomato.

David McKie, The Guardian

Doctor in Trouble

'The trouble with David Owen is that he is the most arrogant

77

politician since Neville Chamberlain,' wrote Joe Haines in the *Daily Mirror*, displaying the adjective that has surely been applied to the SDP leader more times than any other, and probably more to him than any other politician.

Smug, self-satisfied facial expressions and a revelry in showing his undoubted intelligence have made 'Dr Death', as he is known from a mortuary-side manner, one of the most amused politicians at Westminster, if at the same time one of the most respected.

Reported the *Sunday Mirror* with glee: 'Joke: What is the difference between an egg, a drum, and David Owen's ego? You can beat an egg, you can beat a drum, but . . .'

King of the rat pack. Phoney as a nine-pound note.

Dennis Skinner

Superbrat.

David Steel

Likes to pose as Margaret Thatcher in trousers to pick up Tory votes.

Norman Tebbit

Dracula swept-back hair with that glimpse of Mills and Boon grey at the temples, face pasty and peeling as an old billboard with what may have been bits of muesli stuck around his chin, shabby chauffeur's blue suit.

Edward Whitley 'the impertinent interviewer'

Too Hot to Handle

Since she has had the good grace to be a leading contributor to this book, I shall be the last to be hard on the energetic Mrs Edwina Currie, Conservative MP for Derbyshire South, who became a political mega-hate-figure in September 1986 for daring to declare that 'ignorant' Northerners ate too many chips and smoked too much.

Mrs Currie was immediately dubbed 'Vegetable Currie', 'Blunderwoman' (*Daily Mirror*); 'the Princess Michael of Politics' (Keith Waterhouse, *Daily Mail*) and the 'Daughter of Dracula' (Jean Rook, *Daily Express*, with reference to her *Spitting Image* puppet). It was immediately recalled how fellow right-wing Tory MP Mr Tony Marlow had told her: 'We would be grateful if you would leave your jackboots outside before addressing this House.'

She has done for women what Norman Tebbit did for the bicycle.

Liberal Assembly delegate

She has become to the Tory Party what the Bishop of Durham is to the Church of England.

Tory MP Richard Holt

Maggie is but a pale flower compared with this clump of deadly nightshade.

Jean Rook

Already firmly established as the Bernie Grant of conservatism.
David McKie, The Guardian

If I was as skinny as her and looked like a banana, I'd keep my mouth shut.

Cyril Smith

If all this is not praise enough, Mrs Currie scored a sensational success at the subsequent Labour Party conference at Blackpool, managing to draw all fire from Mrs Thatcher by being the target of virtually every speech from the rostrum. Perhaps the most memorable feature of the gathering was the creation of the 'Edwina Currie joke wall' where delegates were invited to scrawl their own slogans in denunciation of her. Some weren't at all bad. Among the best:

No wonder the NHS is short of blood—it's all the black pudding Edwina Currie eats.

Edwina says goblin chips is bad for your elf.

Eat tripe, don't talk it.

If you can't afford Currie, eat the rich.

And:

Edwina, with the cringe on top.

13

Nicknames

One MP was introduced to me (by another Member) as 'The Fastest Willie at Westminster'. I took this to mean he had defeated Lord Whitelaw at one of those inventive Terrace athletic events marshalled by Mr Colin Moynihan, MP. One northern MP, I was told by a Tory back-bencher, is known the length and breadth of the country as 'Shagger'. The reason and derivation perplexes me.

Nicknames abound in politics, partly because of the public school 'club' tradition, partly as a convenient label to identify friends and foes, though mainly, I suspect, as a convenient form of abuse for the overlooked.

Cabinet Table

VISCOUNT WHITELAW
Marshmallow Man
Wobbly Willie

SIR GEOFFREY HOWE
Mr Bumble
The Dead Sheep
Mogadon Man
Sir Godfrey ⎫(*from mis-speak*
Sir Howe-ho⎭*abroad*)
Sir Who?

NIGEL LAWSON
Nasty Nigel
Nero Lawson (*by Neil Kinnock*)
Smuggins (*Westminster School nickname*)

JOHN BIFFEN
Atrocity John
Biffo
The Grand Vizier
John the Baptist

NORMAN FOWLER
Fowlpest
The Thinking Man's Himmler
  (*Channel 4*)

NICHOLAS RIDLEY
Old Neanderthal
Old Nick

NORMAN TEBBIT
All Boots and Braces (*from* Daily Express)
The Chingford Strangler
Darth Vader
Dracula (*'because of his talent for drawing blood', Denis Healey*)
Field Marshal Tebbit (*by Lady Falkender*)
Hound of the Baskervilles
Norman 'Bites Yer Legs' Tebbit (*an allusion to Leeds Utd hard man, Norman Hunter*)

Old Morality (*from* New Statesman)
The Old Ruffian
Piranha (*by John Grant, MP*)
Polecat
Rambo (*from* Daily Mail)
The Unemployment Minister (*from gaffe by BBC's Frances Coverdale*)

KENNETH CLARKE
Piglet
Robin Hood

HE'S NEVER BEEN THE SAME SINCE HE WAS VOTED WET OF THE YEAR

PETER WALKER
The Last Surviving Wet (*from* The Times)
Slater
Worcester Sauce

The Only Man in the Commons with Spray-on Hair (*by Simon Hoggart*)
The Willie Whitelaw of the 1990s (*by Alan Rusbridge*)

KENNETH BAKER
The Avon Man
Mr Chip

JOHN MOORE
Old Moore (*after seer's* Almanac)
The Original Plastic Man

God Bless America

MAYOR DIANNE FEINSTEIN
The Queen of Kook City

SENATOR JOHN GLENN
The Flying Monk

SENATOR GARY HART (that's why he changed his name from Hartpence)
Hot Pants

JEANE KIRKPATRICK
The Unguided Missile (*by Senator Charles Percy*)

WALTER MONDALE
Norwegian Wood

RICHARD PERLE, (Assistant Secretary of Defence)
The Prince of Darkness

RONALD REAGAN
The Great Rondini
Rambo, Ronbo
Rawhide (*Secret Service code name*)
Reagan Hood

DAVID STOCKMAN (ex-US Budget Director)
The Grim Reaper

CASPER WEINBERGER
Cap the Knife
(*And later*) Cap the Ladel

Yes, Minister

DR RHODES BOYSON
Wackford Squeers

EDWINA CURRIE
Cruella de Ville (*from* 101 Dalmatians)
Hot Stuff
The Other Tiresome Woman
La Passionara of Punishment
Princess Pushy
Vegetable Curry (*after North East 'you don't eat right' tour*)
Vindaloo

TIM EGGAR
Frankie Vaughan (*after a facial resemblance*)

TRISTAN GAREL-JONES
Garrulous

DOUGLAS HOGG
Miss Piggy

RICHARD LUCE
Mr Lice (*from press misprint*)

RICHARD NEEDHAM
Knickers (*from a former life selling ladies' underwear at Marks and Spencer*)

JOHN SELWYN-GUMMER
Bummer
Gas 'n' Gaiters
Harpic (*'going round the bend'*)
John Seldon Glummer
Little Gum-Gum
Son of Zorro
The Trojan Pony of the Labour Party

Labour First Team

NEIL KINNOCK
The Boneless Wonder
The Babbling Boyo (*by Jean Rook*)
Hurricane Neil
Neil Bennoch (*by Michael Forsyth, MP*)
The Welsh Windbag
Zanzibar Neil (*by Godfrey Barker*)

ROY HATTERSLEY
Greedy Roy (*from* The Sun)
Heffalump Hattersley (*by Rupert Morris,* Today)
The Mad Hatter (*from* The Sun)
The Michelin Man of British Politics
Mr Punch (*by Geoffrey Dickens*)
Roly-Poly (*from* The Sun)
Vesuvius
The Yorkshire Gasbag (*by Richard Gott: of 'Welsh Windbag'*)

DENIS HEALEY
Denis the Menace
The Steamroller (*by Chris Buckland*)
Thor the God of Thunder (*from* Daily Express)

GERALD KAUFMAN
Baldilocks
Kermit
King Rat (*by Geoffrey Dickens*)

JOHN SMITH
The Bulldozer

MICHAEL MEACHER
The Dalek
Ebenezer Scrooge (*by David McKie*)
Will Hay (*by Geoffrey Dickens*)

International

Boy George — **GEORGE BIRMINGHAM** (Irish Deputy Foreign Minister and 'boy prodigy')

The Bulldozer — **JACQUES CHIRAC**

Baby Doc — **JEAN CLAUDE DUVALIER** (ex-ruler of Haiti)

Iron Maiden of France — **FRANCINE GOMEZ** (leading French businesswoman)

The Silver Bodgie — **ROBERT HAWKE** (after a 1950s Australian Teddy Boy)

Citizen Hersant — **ROBERT HERSANT** (owner of *Le Figaro*)

Lucky Lange — **DAVID LANGE** (after the movie)

The Florentine	FRANÇOIS MITTERAND (after the schemer of Renaissance Italy)
Idi Amin on Valium	ALBERT RENE (Seychelles President)
Dynamite Olga	KARIN SODER (Sweden's first woman party leader)

First Families

The Power behind the Tone	CAROLINE BENN
The All-American Muppet	AMY CARTER
The Steel Magnolia	ROSALYNN CARTER
Big Boss Mama Glenys the Menace Jackie O'Kinnock Mama Kinnock Porky Parry	GLENYS KINNOCK
Nancita The Queen	NANCY REAGAN
Big Denis	DENIS THATCHER

Back-bench Tories

Norman Crumb (*from a mis-hearing*)	MICHAEL ANCRAM
PC Plod (*from* Private Eye)	DR JOHN BLACKBURN
Napoleon Synoddy Titch	PETER BRUINVELS
The Galloping Lawyer	NICK BUDGEN
Winnie the Pooh	WINSTON CHURCHILL
Bunter Buster Snoopy	GEOFFREY DICKENS

Beau Brummell Dandy Nick The Maharajah	NICHOLAS FAIRBAIRN
Basil Brush The Cheeky Chappie The Shipley Strangler	SIR MARCUS FOX
The Coppers' Bark	SIR ELDON GRIFFITHS
Bertie Wooster	TOBY JESSEL
Silent Knight	GREGORY KNIGHT
Buffalo Jill	MRS JILL KNIGHT
The Boers' Bore	IAN LLOYD
The Buchan Bulldog	ALBERT MCQUARRIE
Dormouse	TIM SAINSBURY
Bunter King of the Parliamentary Wallies (*by Simon Hoggart*)	NICHOLAS SOAMES
Full Steen Ahead Sleepyhead	ANTHONY STEEN

Angel Delight (*from being made
  almost an 'Instant Whip' on
  entering Parliament*)
	SIR JOHN STRADLING-THOMAS

Globe Trotter (*a reference to frequent foreign travel*)	NEVILLE TROTTER
The Bishop	SIR WILLIAM VAN STRAUBENZEE
Biggles	BILL WALKER
Junket Jerry (*from* Private Eye)	JERRY WIGGIN
The Macclesfield Volcano Rentaquote John Wayne	NICHOLAS WINTERTON
Yo-Yo	TIM YEO

Labour Benches

Screaming Ron Brown	RON BROWN (Leith)

The Laird of the Binns Lone Ranger of the Labour Party	TAM DALYELL
The Battling Butterball The Bouncing Butterball Gun Boats	GWYNETH DUNWOODY
Ms Hairperson	HARRIET HARMAN
The Scottish Werewolf	JOHN MAXTON
Man Friday (*by Edward Pearce*)	BILL MICHIE
Cro-Magnon Man Dracula's Valet The Hard Man of Hackney	BRIAN SEDGEMORE
The Duchess	RENEE SHORT
The Beast of Bolsover Dennis the Menace The Hooligan Royal Old Yellow Socks	DENNIS SKINNER

Loose Alliance

Val Taddino (Liberator *anagram*)	DAVID ALTON
Dandy Podwash (Liberator *anagram*)	PADDY ASHDOWN
Dogger Bank Trawler (*'as wet as the North Sea'*)	CHRISTOPHER BROCKLEBANK-FOWLER (defector to SDP)
Mabel McClour (Liberator *anagram*)	MALCOLM BRUCE
Edward VII Merle de Funct (Liberator *anagram*)	CLEMENT FREUD
The Robert Mitchum of the Sheep Fells (*by Michael White*) The Welsh Mountain	GERAINT HOWELLS
Joy Skinner (Liberator *anagram*) Smoothiechops Taffy (*by Neil Kinnock*) Woy	ROY JENKINS

Elena Hendrykes (Liberator *anagram*) — CHARLES KENNEDY

Silvia D. Cherry (Liberator *anagram*) — RICHARD LIVSEY

Doomwatch Macferlie (Liberator *anagram*)
Mr Dial-a-quote — MICHAEL MEADOWCROFT

Dawn Video (Liberator *anagram*)
Dr David Bore (*Colin Welch*)
Doctor Death
Doctor Smug (*from* The Sun)
East Ender
Maggie Thatcher in Trousers — DAVID OWEN

King Kong — CYRIL SMITH

Bossy Boots
Boy David
Divey Stalin (*translation to Gaelic*)
Eva Tiddles (Liberator *anagram*)
The Microchap — DAVID STEEL

The Archangel Shirley
The Belgian Lieutenant's Woman (*by Frank Johnson after 'Woy's' translation to Brussels*)
Goody Two Shoes
I Whirl Aimlessly (*anagram*)
Shilly Shally Shirl (*from* The Sun) — SHIRLEY WILLIAMS

Belly Dancer
Finnegan's Wake (*after defeated Tory opponent*) — IAN WRIGGLESWORTH

In the Wings

Lady Forkbender (*from* Private Eye) — MARCIA, LADY FALKENDER

The Foghorn
Witch-finder General — JOHN GOLDING

Beau Derek
The Militant Maggot (*by Neil Kinnock*) — DEREK HATTON

88

The Hack Saw (*reputation for 'cutting up' the press*) Salty (*after a liking for fish and chips*) The Yorkshire Rasputin	BERNARD INGHAM (Prime Minister's Press Secretary)
The Big Fella The Devil	IAN PAISLEY
Brown Owl	ENOCH POWELL
The Devil's Disciple	PETER ROBINSON
Son of Thatcher (*by Lord Murray of Epping Forest*)	ARTHUR SCARGILL
Pipsqueak Pete (*from* The Sun)	PETER TATCHELL
The Merioneth Marxist (*by Neil Kinnock*)	DAFYDD ELIS THOMAS

Temporarily Out to Grass

Bennatollah Dreamer (*early nickname*) Hover Benn	TONY BENN
The Beast with the Living Eyebrows (*by Chris Buckland*)	LEON BRITTAN
Dixon of Dock Green Policeman Jim Stoker Jim	JIM CALLAGHAN
Gipsy Rose Foot Rip Van Foot The Old Grey Sheep ('*not smart enough to be the fox*') Worzel Gummidge	MICHAEL FOOT
Supergrass (*from days as PPS to Mrs Thatcher*)	IAN GOW
The Mushroom Man (*as Labour's Deputy Chief Whip: 'keep 'em in the dark and smother them with manure*')	WALTER HARRISON

Dame Evita	DAME JUDITH HART
Ted Vicious (*Frank Johnson*) The Grocer The Old Pretender	EDWARD HEATH
Benito Fog on the Mersey Goldilocks Sir Jasper Lord Liverpool Golden Wonder	MICHAEL HESELTINE
Blue Ken	PATRICK JENKIN

Mephistopheles Incarnate
    (*National Association of Teachers*)
Sir Sheath Joseph (*for advocating
    less freedom while Health
    Secretary*)
Smokey Joe
	SIR KEITH JOSEPH

Napoleon	ROY MASON
Rip Van Winkle	LORD MULLEY
Mr Silvikrin	CECIL PARKINSON
Pussyfoot Prior (*from* Daily Express)	JAMES PRIOR

The Grand Old Duke of York (*On
    'Centre Forward', 'He marched
    them up to the top of the hill,' etc.*)
Mr Yesterday
	FRANCIS PYM

The Blessed Norman St John the Divine Pope Norman	NORMAN ST JOHN STEVAS

Dog Eats Dog

PC Callaghan (*by Michael Foot*)	JAMES CALLAGHAN
Kermit (*by Norman St John Stevas*)	LORD CARRINGTON
Geoffrey Who? (*by Sir Ian Gilmour*)	SIR GEOFFREY HOWE

Le Roi Jean Quinze (*by David Owen*)	ROY JENKINS
Kilroy-Sulk (*by Labour MPs*)	ROBERT KILROY-SILK
On-goose (*by Sir Ian Gilmour*)	SIR ANGUS MAUDE
Harold's Lapdog (*by Denis Healey*)	PETER SHORE
Chief Strangler (*by Julian Critchley*) The Prince of Darkness (*by Julian Critchley*)	NORMAN TEBBIT

14

Hecklers Beware

HECKLER TO SIR ROBERT MENZIES: Tell us all you know, Bob—it won't take long.
MENZIES: I'll tell you everything we both know—it won't take any longer.

Heckling is a traditional, integral and often essential ingredient in the successful public meeting. According to Norman Tebbit: 'Good heckling makes a speech, because the worst thing of all is to have an audience that just sits there like a great pudding. If somebody in the audience begins to question or heckle it is marvellous, because you have a contact with the audience and it can become great fun.'

One of the best answers to hecklers I heard in recent years was at a meeting in Rhyader, Powys, during the Brecon and Radnor by-election. A Labour supporter protested loudly that stewards were trying to force him to remove his trilby. The speaker, Mr Michael Heseltine, singled the dissident out and said:

I know why you don't want to take off your hat. It's because there's absolutely nothing underneath it! [Collapse of audience.]

I also liked the unexpected interruption to the SDP conference revue in Harrogate in 1986. One of the stage characters had asked: 'What have the Liberals got that we haven't got?' Back came the response from one wag in the auditorium: 'MPs!'

Most active politicians have a favourite heckling story to tell:

PETER ARCHER, QC, MP
Warley West (Lab)

I was once involved in the following exchange:

92

HECKLER: If Shakespeare were alive today he would have voted Tory.

PA: If Shakespeare were alive today he would have been so old that we would have forgiven him anything.

MADAM YOU COULD CHARM THE BIRDS OFF THE TREES

GEOFFREY DICKENS, MP
Littleborough and Saddleworth (C)

HECKLER: You are two faced!

GD: Would I be wearing this face if I had two?

TOM ELLIS
SDP Candidate for Clwyd South West
former MP for Wrexham

A Conservative back-bencher shouted to Michael Foot, who was making a speech on the European Community: 'That's only words!'

Foot replied: 'What do you expect, algebra?'

JOHN GOLDING
General Secretary, National Communications Union,
former MP for Newcastle-under-Lyme (Lab)

In the 1970 election campaign a Tory girl was sent round to plague me by asking awkward questions at my meetings. At the second meeting she said: 'Look, all these people here are in favour of hanging,' pointing to the audience. 'How can you justify voting against capital punishment?'

I replied: 'Look, love, with my luck if I voted for hanging on a Friday I'd be the first to go on the Monday!'

IAN MIKARDO, MP
Bow and Poplar (Lab)

At an open-air trade union recruitment meeting in Bedford in 1944 (not long after Ernest Bevin's Regulation 1AA, which many trade unionists objected to) I was continually asked by a man just below me: 'Wot abaht Ernie Bevin?'

Finally, I leaned over and asked: 'Wot abaht 'im?'

This answer seemed completely to satisfy the questioner.

GERRY NEALE, MP
Cornwall North (C)

Peter Walker in North Cornwall: 'A vote for Gerry Neale is a vote for common sense.'

'Rubbish,' came from a heckler, untidy and dishevelled.

'The gentleman there says "rubbish", and he looks a good judge of that.'

DAVID STEEL
Leader of the Liberal Party

I tend to ignore hecklers but I admire the way that American Presidential candidate Adlai Stevenson is said to have dealt with one. Having stated that he would always be a Democrat, since his grandfather and father had been Democrats, a heckler demanded what he would be if his grandfather and father had been jackasses. 'A Republican,' was Adlai Stevenson's reply

NORMAN TEBBIT
Chairman of the Conservative Party

My favourite way to deal with hecklers is to lead them on and use them to make my own point. An extreme example was a meeting in Manchester when I was Secretary of State for Employment. There were a large number from the extreme left, not heckling but trying to prevent me from being heard at all. They were of the 'Gissus a job' militant wing, led by a scruffy female whose harridan screeches were punctuated with

94

obscenities. I waited until the audience was sick of her, and then turned on her. 'You madam—what did you say?' 'Gissus a job.' 'Madam, you're dirty, you're filthy, you're unkempt, you're foulmouthed and disgusting—why should anyone in their right mind give you a job?' The audience cheered, the hecklers fell silent and slunk away.

JOHN WATSON, MP
Skipton and Ripon (C)

In 1975 I was speaking at a public meeting in Bentham, North Yorkshire, during one of the more vigorous episodes of the Cod War. One questioner asked me why we, a great seafaring nation, were allowing ourselves to be pushed around by these upstart Icelanders. 'Well,' I replied, 'things will improve now—we're sending in the Royal Navy.'

'Aye,' came the call from the back of the hall, 'and how much bloody fish are they going to catch?'

It's My Shout

Here is the professionals' advice on how to deal with troublesome interrupters:

RON BROWN, MP
Leith (Lab)

Say: 'Sorry, I missed that—could you speak up a bit?'

KEN CURE
AUEW, and member of
Labour's National Executive

At a meeting in Birmingham I managed to squash a heckler with: 'Please don't interrupt me while I'm interrupting you!'

ILLTYD HARRINGTON
former Deputy Leader of the GLC

Charm.

LORD JENKINS OF PUTNEY
former Labour Minister for the Arts

Hand them the mike.

IAN MIKARDO, MP
Bow and Poplar (Lab)

I never reply to hecklers until they've put their point three times.

DAVID MUDD, MP
Falmouth and Camborne (C)

Patent remedy: develop a hearing defect.

TONY SPELLER, MP
Devon North (C)

When heckled, I always wave dismissively and say 'I've been heckled by experts,' which always annoys!

IVOR STANBROOK, MP
Orpington (C)

If persistent, I tell the audience that I am letting them into a secret. 'We thought the meeting would be dull, so we hired our friend to liven things up. I hope you think he's worth the money.'

DAVID TRIPPIER, MP
Rossendale and Darwen (C)

I usually find that hecklers move with me from one meeting to another, so I offer to give them a lift.

15

I've Never Been So Insulted . . .

God help anyone who gets in her way.
Republican Congresswoman Bobbi Fielder
on Geraldine Ferraro

In a phrase . . . reputations are despatched. A selection of the cutest, and meanest, cruel shots of all:

TONY BENN	Barmy.	*Jim Prior*
	Doomed to political extinction.	*Winston Churchill MP*
RHODES BOYSON	A man who thinks flowers grow by night.	*Neil Kinnock*
JIM CALLAGHAN	The man of indecision.	*Edward Heath*
MICHAEL FOOT	Jekyll and Hyde.	*Lady Falkender*
COLONEL GADDAFI	A mad dog.	*President Reagan*
	Let's put him back in his box.	*George Shultz*

A DOUBLE ORDER OF SACKCLOTH AND ASHES PLEASE.. WE'VE HAD A BAD GO OF SELF-ABASEMENT

ROY HATTERSLEY	Voice like the last splash in a soda syphon.	*Jock Bruce-Gardyne*
BOB HAWKE	Splattering us with bullshit.	*Patrick White*
DENIS HEALEY	The atomic maniac.	Pravda
	A political thug.	*Lady Falkender*
EDWARD HEATH	No political antennae.	*Cecil King*
MICHAEL HESELTINE	Rabble rouser to the gentry.	*Simon Hoggart*
	The yearly man.	*Frank Johnson*
ROY JENKINS	He was born old.	*Lord Wilson*
SIR KEITH JOSEPH	The thinking man's Rhodes Boyson.	*Neil Kinnock*
NEIL KINNOCK	The Nowhere Man.	The Sun
	The wet, windy, Welsh waffler.	*Sir John Junor*
KEN LIVINGSTONE	The poor man's Benn.	*Paul Johnson*
BRIAN MULRONEY	Waffling.	Time *magazine*
DAVID OWEN	All at sea.	*Denzil Davies*
RONALD REAGAN	Herbert Hoover with a smile.	*Tip O'Neill*
JOHN SELWYN-GUMMER	A crystallized choirboy.	*Julian Critchley*
	A political pipsqueak.	*Gerald Kaufman ('Yes, but that presupposes he has pips to squeak'—Lady Falkender)*
RICHARD WAINWRIGHT	Looks more and more like a Toby jug.	*Derek Brown,* The Guardian
DEIRDRE WOOD	Godzilla.	London Daily News

An Indispensable
A–Z of Up-to-date Insults

The official candidates' self-help guide of untried invective should give you the edge in any political contest.

But first, some useful devices to help you construct your own gems of vitriol:

Similes are perhaps the most ready resort: 'as much grace as a camel with halitosis', 'cold as a cod on ice', 'as lazy as a tortoise on valium', 'unobtrusive as an atom bomb test', 'useful as a cast-iron parachute'. Experiment with these introductions: Smile like . . ., Nerve like . . ., Brains like . . ., Speaks like . . ., Principles like. . . .

Alliteration gives an extra boost, witness Safire's 'nattery nabobs of negativism' and Norman Tebbit's 'bigots for the big battalions' (union leaders). Try 'the Michelangelo of the main chance', 'the Rt Hon Member for Mendacity', 'the Ministerial Muffin the Mule'.

Substitution is one of the favourite resorts of the wit, and much seen in quotation books. Here one word or syllable of a popular phrase or saying is substituted to alter the meaning and suggest deep and lasting insight (I've always thought this was a little of a cheat!): 'On a whinge and a prayer', 'His facts are worse than his diction', 'When is the time he ever came to the aid of the party', 'Foot in the mouth and fancy free', 'Star of the partly pontificial broadcast'.

Allusion to historical figures I consider overblown, particularly old favourites like Pétain, Attila, Genghis Khan, Goebbels, etc. My advice would be to go in for ethnological and geological slurs (which not only sound mightily impressive, they give a lasting hint of scholarship). 'Antediluvian' and 'Neanderthal' have been overused; and Teddy Roosevelt pinched the best with 'pithecanthropoid' (= ape man) But why not try: amphigamous (without distinct sexual organs); emphoteric (acting both ways); antemundane (pre-creation); anthropoid (apelike); batrachian (frog-

99

like); colubrine (snakelike); ichthyoid (fishlike); malacostracan (crablike); Ogygian (obscurely prehistoric); ophidian (snakelike); Palaeolithic (Stone Age); Palaeozoic (belonging to the most primitive form of life); passerine (sparrowlike); prehensile (grasping); primeval, primordial ('with twice the slime'?), Proterozoic (primitive); therianthropic (with both animal and human characteristics); theriomorphic (having animal form); ursine (bearlike).

Topicality: Much public credence will come from the skilful introduction of 'vogue' topics and characters, particularly from television: 'All the slyness of J.R. Ewing, with none of the style.' 'Combines the humility of Derek Hatton with the foresight of Arthur Scargill.' 'The only man in love with his own *Spitting Image* puppet.'

Using Christian names as a base for your insult is often highly successful, e.g. 'Way above the Norm', 'Hectoring Tone', 'Marge Thatcher, the original agony aunt'.

Other useful constructions include the literary scenario (many variations possible): 'He has two books in his library, and he hasn't finished colouring one of them.' Q. 'Shall we give him a book for his birthday?' A. 'He's got one of those already.' Reincarnation: 'If he believed in reincarnation he'd come back as a (leech, gin and tonic, Jeffrey Archer's accountant, etc). When he grows up: 'When he grows up he wants to (be able to read and write, enter politics, learn the difference between right and wrong).' Alter ego: 'His alter ego is (a snake, worm, General Pinochet's helmet, Derek Hatton's ventriloquist, etc).'

Also worth experimenting with is Harold Wilson's celebrated Macmillan jibe: 'He had an expensive education, Eton and Suez.' You could usefully make that Caerphilly and Goose Green, Haberdashers' and the IMF, Magdalen and Pretoria, Tory Central Office and Victoria Station, or whatever.

The guide that follows really speaks for itself: merely identify the characteristics of your opponent from the list on the left and build up your own store of venom. For convenience rather than chauvinism we have assumed your opponent is male. Otherwise naturally use 'she' for 'he', 'her' for 'him' etc.

Accident-prone:	The only man to throw banana skins in front of him wherever he goes.
Adolescent:	Peter Panic.
	Still living off his Yuppie fat.
Aged:	He's already been declared an ancient monument—Grade III, of no particular merit.
	My favourite local antiquity.

Airy-fairy: The Heath Robinson of politics: every construction ingenious but utterly unworkable.

Amorous: He doesn't like holidays, all that lying around or playing. He prefers the rest of the year. All that playing around and lying.

THE BACKBENCHERS WERE RESTLESS TONIGHT

Bearded: Thinks hirsuiteness is a substitute for astuteness.

Bellicose: An Ian Botham approach to politics . . . slog 'em and s** 'em.

Blustering: The politics of a bat: blind, bleating and permanently looking at the world upside down.

He may have more than one string to his bow, but he cannot play a tune on any of them.

The original cloud in cuckoo land.

Boring: The original square on the hypotenuse.

Bumptious: A living pompromise.

Capricious: Straight as a concertina, and available to play just as many tunes.

He once stood on his principles. They were so badly trampled he has never bothered since.

Combative: Like the Chinese sex maniac, there's nothing he likes more than an election.

Conceited:	Everything about him is swell, particularly that part of him between the ears.
Corpulent:	The original lead balloon.
	Living proof of massive inflation.
Daffy:	He once stood in the same election as Screaming Lord Sutch . . . everyone was confused. Nobody could tell which was the real Monster Raving Loony.
Decrepit:	Brinking on the tottering.
	The creaking gate who hangs long on his whinges.
	They say there's no fool like an old fool, and he certainly fills the job description.
Dense:	So many bats in his belfry, they slapped an environmental protection order on him.
Dim-witted:	The only politician to be declared an education-free zone.
Disloyal:	Backs his colleagues to the hilt . . . the knife already being in their backs.
	Would follow his leader to the edge of any cliff, and then push her over.
Disruptive:	Is to politics what a London cabbie is to traffic.
Dissembling:	Tarpaulin man—he's always trying to cover things up.
Droning:	Forever bleating about the bush.
Dull:	Like the typical British weather forecast: wet and windy.
	He asked a colleague for a character reference and was told 'How can I? You haven't got one.'
Egg-headed:	His best friend's a computer.
	The most brilliant man of his day. And his day was 21 April 1941.
Egotistical:	Invites his friends around every Ascension Day as if something important is going to happen.
	Has adopted a theme tune: 'Amazing Grace, How Great Thou Art.'
	All pomp and no circumstance.
Employment Minister:	Seasonally maladjusted.

Empty-headed:	Thinks pragmatism is an aching disease of the joints.
	A man of fresh ideas, every one with the heady aroma of a day out in the country.
Equivocal:	The Hon Member for no man's land.
Excitable:	Frenzied as a cat plugged into a 240-volt socket.
Extreme right:	A dedicated follower of Fascism.
Fallen:	Wrecked on the Tarpeian rocks of his own ambition.
	Opportunity knocked.
Fence-sitting:	Always takes up a Grand Central Station.
	The original ornamental hedge.
	A hands-on politician: on the one hand, on the other hand, on the one hand, on the other hand.
	If he auditioned to be part of a pantomime horse he'd want to be one front leg and one back leg.
Foolish:	Gravity's answer to rising damp.
	Wet as a glass of stagnant pondwater, but only half as interesting.
	The Prime Minister/party leader's noodle.
Fun-loving:	He's the man who put the shadow into the Shadow Cabinet.
Garrulous:	The only man the Blarney Stone tried to kiss instead of vice versa.
	The only man who can turn a point of order into the Sermon on the Mount.
Grasping:	Always willing to lend a hand—providing it is to put in your pockets.
Gross:	A walking advertisement for conspicuous consumption.
	Self-mocked by his own enormity.
	Fileofats.
Imitative:	His friends call him 'photocopy'—he's never once in his life been original.
Inanimate:	A first-class mind in a second-class compartment.
	They organized a search party for his intellect, but had to call it off.
	If there was VAT on intelligence, he'd be zero rated.

Incompetent:	The nine day's blunder.
	His constituency party must have been early birds indeed to catch such a worm.
Ineffectual:	He put the wimp into whimpering.
Left-wing:	The only man to nominate Stalin for the Nobel Peace Prize.
	The original red herring.
Malevolent:	A political virus: always trying to catch you unawares and make you suffer.
Medical:	One doctor who can't bury his mistakes—they're all there in Hansard.
	The original Hippocratic oaf.
Monotonous:	Universally acknowledged as the Commons whine expert.
Muddle-headed:	The only man to keep his nose firmly to the ground and his ears to the grindstone.
	He suffers fools gladly, mainly because they make him feel so much at home.
Narcissistic:	His relationship with his bathroom mirror will surely go down as one of the great love stories of history.
	A man with a great vision, but sadly only of himself.
Narrow-minded:	His mind is so closed you would need a crowbar to open it.
Obese:	He put the podge in 'hodge-podge'.
	The original hot-air balloon.
Ostentatious:	A smarty-boots in fancy pants . . . with his knickers permanently in a twist.
Overenthusiastic:	Like a man on an exercise bicycle: he puts in a lot of effort, but you know he isn't going anywhere.
	The Abominable Snowman of politics: half man, half bear; rare, elusive; and spends all his time climbing mountains.
Past it:	One foot in the grave, the other firmly in his mouth.
Pugilistic:	Doesn't like to kick a man while he's down. He prefers to stand on his throat instead.
Reactionary:	Makes Alf Garnett look like Florence Nightingale.
	The blimp leading the blind.

Reticent:	The tic-tac man of politics: furious at giving signals but never keen to open his mouth.
	A political semaphore: he talks in smoke signals.
	I'm not saying he's timid, but he was heckled once and cried for a fortnight.
Right-wing:	The original knee-jerk reactionary.
	He's setting up a new charity: War *and* Want.
Ruthless:	A Mantovani politician: everything comes with strings.
	A man with so many double-crosses to bear.
Scheming:	Innocuous as sin. A paradox of virtue.
	Gelignite wouldn't melt in his mouth.
	He has but one game: swallow my leader.
Scruffy:	Combines Michael Foot's dress sense with Shirley Williams' skill with the comb.
	The only MP to miss the Queen's Speech for a jumble sale.
Shrill:	Pre-hysterical.
Silly:	Proof that not every clown has a silver lining.
Socialist:	Remember, the redder the rose, the more soil (fertilizer, manure etc.) around the roots.
Spluttering:	Like an aerosol can of shaving foam, he froths uncontrollably, only at the end to expire in an orgy of gas.
Superficial:	Politics like curry: it seems hot and spicy today, but you pay tomorrow.
	His colleagues call him skipper—he skips this problem, he skips that problem.
	Certain of everything, but informed of nothing.
	A parliamentary G-string—he's always so scantily briefed.
Swell-headed:	He's not vain, just prematurely celestial.
Sycophantic:	The first professional climber whose feet have yet to leave the ground.
	Always ready with a kind word for his superiors.
Thin:	Little Will O' the Wimp.
Treasury, at the:	Look at the economy under him—it's groan and groan.

Trotskyist:	Thinks Bernie Grant's a dangerous Liberal. His favourite aperitif is a Molotov cocktail.
Ubiquitous:	He is to politics what the Dimblebys are to television: you get the impression that there's no getting away from him.
Uncaring:	The first man the caring society ever turned down for membership.
	His motto: a friend in need is no friend of mine.
	Still thinks the Good Samaritan should have been arrested for loitering.
	Thinks Compassion is a Soviet bloc trade organization.
Unctuous:	Prefers blarney to barney.
Undernourished:	One rake who'll never progress.
	The walking slide rule: but can you really count on him?
Ungifted:	A Tippex politician, forever trying to white out his own incompetence.
	His biggest break in politics is likely to be 57 in the Commons snooker room.
Unlikeable:	Like comparisons, he is odious.
	Known to his friends as fishbone, from the way he always sticks in your throat.
Unoriginal:	The Anne Robinson of politics: always reciting someone else's points of view.
Unpleasant:	Grows on you like ring-worm.
	He's one of life's little animosities.
	What can you say to him except: 'Go forth and visit the taxidermist.'
Unpopular:	His colleagues feel about him much the same as turkeys must feel about Bernard Matthews.
	His constituency party is forming an escape committee.
Unpredictable:	A political geyser: long periods of silence punctuated by sporadic blasts of hot air.
Unprepossessing:	Thinks the Fourth Estate is a council house complex in Sheffield.
Untrustworthy:	A political magpie, nest stuffed with others' trinkets.
Untruthful:	His own personal computer wouldn't accept any data he tried to log in. It kept flashing up a message: 'I DON'T BELIEVE YOU.'

Vain:	Preens himself like a peacock, crows like a cock-a-doodle-doo, and deserves to be given the bird.
Warmongering:	Never saw a brink without trying to teeter on it. His ambition is to be aboard the first Cruise missile into Moscow. So much a hawk he has to go once a month to have his talons trimmed. The only man to escalate a game of solitaire.
Wavering:	The horns of every dilemma. He's on the border of everything ridiculous.
Welsh:	Lily-liver of the valleys. The ever-sprouting leak.
Wooden:	At every meeting where he speaks they hold a raffle. It's known as 'sweeping the bored'.

But watch out, of course, for the cruellest barb of all: 'Yes, I like that. I liked it when I first read it in *The Official Candidate's Book of Political Insults!!*'

Select Bibliography

Barrett, Lawrence I. *Gambling with History: Reagan in the White House* (Doubleday, New York, 1983)

Behrens, Robert. *The Conservative Party from Heath to Thatcher* (Saxon House, Farnborough, 1980)

Blake, Robert. *Disraeli* (Eyre and Spottiswoode, 1966)

Campbell, John. *Roy Jenkins. A Biography* (Weidenfeld and Nicolson, 1983)

Carvel, John. *Citizen Ken* (Chatto and Windus, 1984)

Celebrity Research Group. *The Bedside Book of Celebrity Gossip* (Prince Paperbacks, New York, 1984)

Colquohoun, Maureen. *A Woman in the House* (Scan Books, 1980)

Critchley, Julian. *Westminster Blues: Minor Chords* (Elm Tree Books, 1985)

Doxat, John. *Shinwell Talking* (Burlington Press, Cambridge, 1984)

Drew, Elizabeth. *Portrait of an Election: The 1980 American Presidential Campaign* (Routledge and Kegan Paul, 1981)

Ferraro, Geraldine A. *Ferraro: My Story* (Bantam, New York, 1985)

Fisher, Nigel. *The Tory Leaders* (Weidenfeld and Nicolson, 1977)

Foot, Michael. *Another Heart and Other Pulses* (Collins, 1984)

Foot, Michael. *Loyalists and Loners* (Collins, 1986)

Harbaugh, William H. *The Life and Times of Theodore Roosevelt* (Oxford University Press, New York, 1961)

Hoggart, Simon. *On the House* (Robson, 1981)

Hoggart, Simon. *Back on the House* (Robson, 1982)

Hoggart, Simon. *House of Ill Fame* (Robson, 1985)

Johnson, Frank. *Out of Order* (Robson, 1982)

Johnson, Frank. *Election Year* (Robson, 1983)

Jones, Graham. *Forked Tongues: The Book of Lies, Half Truths and Excuses* (Century, 1984)

Jones, Graham. *Own Goals: A Devastating Collection of Self-inflicted Disasters, Blunders and Super-Goofs* (Century, 1985)

Jones, Graham. *The Forked Tongues Annual* (Century, 1985)

Jones, Graham. *I Don't Hate Men But . . ./I Don't Hate Women But . . .* (Century, 1986)

Junor, John. *The Best of JJ* (Sidgwick and Jackson, 1981)

Kaufman, Gerald. *How to be a Minister* (Sidgwick and Jackson, 1980)

Kronenberger, Louis. *The Cutting Edge* (Doubleday, New York, 1970)

Mitchell, Austin. *Four Years in the Death of the Labour Party* (Methuen, 1983)

Mitchell, Austin. *Westminster Man* (Methuen, 1982)
Morris, Edmund. *The Rise of Theodore Roosevelt* (Collins, 1979)
Pearce, Edward. *The Senate of Lilliput* (Faber and Faber, 1983)
Pearce, Edward. *Hummingbirds and Hyenas* (Faber and Faber, 1985)
Perry, Ronald. *The Programming of the President* (Aurun Press, 1984)
Phillips, Melanie. *The Divided House: Women at Westminster* (Sidgwick and Jackson, 1980)
Robinson, Ray. *The Wit of Sir Robert Menzies* (Leslie Frewin, 1966)
Roth, Andrew *Parliamentary Profiles* (4 vol) (Parliamentary Profiles, 1984)
Smith, Cyril. *Big Cyril: The Autobiography of Cyril Smith* (W. H. Allen, 1977)
Stockman, David A. *The Triumph of Politics* (The Bodley Head, 1986)
Tatchell, Peter. *The Battle for Bermondsey* (Heretic Books, 1984)
Young, Hugo and Sloman, Anne. *The Thatcher Phenomenon* (BBC, 1986)

Grateful Thanks . . .

Firstly, I must not insult Sarah Wallace of Century Hutchinson by failing to reveal that she is the brains who thought up this most vicious of compilations.

Secondly, a sincere and profound thanks to the politicians and trade union leaders who contributed, and their staff. Those to whom I can express gratitude publicly are: Rt Hon Peter Archer, QC, MP; Paddy Ashdown, MP; Henry Bellingham, MP; Rt Hon Lord Beswick, PC, JP; Sydney Bidwell, MP; Lord Brockway; Ron Brown, MP; Sydney Chapman, MP; Bob Cryer, MEP; Ken Cure; Edwina Currie, MP; Tam Dalyell, MP; Geoffrey Dickens, MP; Mrs Helena Dightam; Lord James Douglas-Hamilton, MP; John Edmonds; Tom Ellis; Nicholas Fairbairn of Fordell, QC, MP; Baroness Faithfull, OBE; Alex Falconer, MEP; Rt Hon Earl Ferrers, Bt, PC, DL; Rt Hon Michael Foot, PC, MP; George Foulkes, JP, MP; John Golding; Sir Eldon Griffiths, MP; Illtyd Harrington; Jerry Hayes, MP; Richard Heller; Robert Hicks, MP; Lord Jenkins of Putney; Tim Luckhurst; Patrick McNair-Wilson, MP; John McWilliam, MP; Joan Maynard, MP; Ian Mikardo, MP; David Mudd, MP; Rt Hon Lord Murray of Epping Forest, OBE, PC; Gerry Neale, MP; Matthew Parris; Rt Hon James Prior, PC, MP; Stephen Ross, MP; Len Scott; Sir Michael Shaw, JP, DL, MP; Bill Sirs, JP; Tony Speller, MP; Ivor Stanbrook, MP; Lord Strabolgi; Rt Hon Norman Tebbit, PC, MP; David Trippier, JP, MP; Baroness Trumpington of Sandwich; Graham Watson; John Watson, MP; Ian Wilson and Sir Philip Goodhart, MP.

This project could not have been undertaken without reference to some eleven national daily newspapers and eight national Sundays; *Time* and *Newsweek*. I would like to thank the publishers of some 250 books on politics whose chapters I scoured for material favourite or forgotten. The main sources are listed in a select bibliography. Anyone insulted at being omitted is invited to contact the publishers for inclusion in subsequent editions.

Finally, sincere thanks to my wife Lynne who carried out the newspaper library research and, with only the occasional flurry of abuse to the typewriter, carried out much of the hard work.